"IN HIS OWN LANGUAGE"

Redd
Center
Publications

"IN HIS OWN LANGUAGE"

Mormon Spanish Speaking Congregations in the United States

*

Jessie L. Embry

The Charles Redd Center for Western Studies
Brigham Young University
Provo, Utah
1997

Redd Center Publications are made possible by a grant from Charles Redd. This grant served as the basis for the establishment of the Charles Redd Center for Western Studies at Brigham Young University.

Center editor: William A. Wilson

ISBN 1–56085–092–2 (pbk.)

LIBRARY OF CONGRESS CATALOGING-IN-PUBLICATION DATA

Embry, Jessie L.–
In his own language : Mormon Spanish-speaking congregations in the United States / Jessie L. Embry.
p. cm.
Includes index.
1. Ethnic relations—Religious aspects—Church of Jesus Christ of Latter-Day Saints. 2. Ethnic relations—Religious aspects—Mormon Church. 3. Church of Jesus Christ of Latter-Day Saints—Membership. 4. Mormon Church—Membership. 5. Church of Jesus Christ of Latter-Day Saints—Relations. 6. Mormon Church—Relations.
I. Title. II. Series.
BX8643.E43 1997
289.3′73′08968—dc21 97–33757
CIP

"In His Own Language" was printed on acid-free paper meeting the permanence of paper requirements of the American National Standard for Information Sciences. The book was composed, printed, and bound in the United States of America.

First Printing, 1997.

Distributed by Signature Books, 564 West 400 North, Salt Lake City, Utah 84116

To My Parents

Bertis L. and Anna E. C. Embry

for their loving support

For it shall come to pass in that day,

that every man shall hear

the fulness of the gospel in his own tongue,

and in his own language, . . .

—D&C 90:11

CONTENTS

ACKNOWLEDGMENTS

My father has always had a great love for the people of Latin America. Believing that he had a religious opportunity to work with the native people of Central and South America, he taught himself Spanish and then looked for chances to use his language and technical skills as an irrigation engineer in those countries. My father and mother lived in Guatemala where my father helped small farmers grow crops year round. While there he also worked closely with the LDS mission. Because of their love for the Latino people and their support for me throughout my life, I am dedicating this monograph to them.

The LDS Ethnic Oral History Project has given me an increased awareness of the needs of various ethnic groups in the United States. This monograph is based on the interviews in the LDS Hispanic American Oral History Project, but all of the interviews in the LDS German-speaking, LDS Native American, LDS Asian American, LDS Polynesian American, and LDS African American Oral History Projects helped me develop the information for this study.

This monograph would not be possible without the help of many people. The College of Family, Home, and Social Sciences and the Religious Studies Center at Brigham Young University helped fund some of the oral history projects. I am especially grateful for the financial support of the Charles Redd Center for Western Studies. Directors Thomas G. Alexander, William A. "Bert" Wilson, and Edward A. Geary trusted me to pick good research topics and supported me in many ways. Kris Nelson, the Redd Center secretary, listened to my stories, processed interviews, read drafts, and gave me needed encouragement.

I have enjoyed working with and becoming friends with the BYU students who helped in the LDS Hispanic Oral History Project. Esmeralda Meraz Amos, Katuska Serrano, and Andrea Van Wagenen conducted most of the oral history interviews. Janean Goodsell Baker also talked to Latino American Mormons in Washington, D.C. Their efforts to find, contact, and then interview the people made this book possible.

After the interviews were conducted, Kim Turner Blight, Kim Snow, Elaine Campbell, and Rachel Nathan transcribed the English interviews. I am especially grateful for those who helped me with the Spanish interviews. Olga de la Rosa transcribed, Rebecca Ream Vorimo edited, and Esmeralda Meraz Amos proofread them. Then Jerry Gowen, Ellen Morgan, and Anna Morgan read through the interviews and translated the information that I needed.

Others helped me find needed material. The material at the LDS Church Historical Department was very valuable. The interviews that Gordon Irving and William G. Hartley conducted in the 1970s gave me important data. My friends Ron Watt, Michael Landon, Chad Orton, and Matt Heiss who work at the Historical Department have always helped me find additional information.

I appreciate those who read drafts and helped in editing and refining my ideas. These include John Sillito, my sister Janet Embry, Lavina Fielding Anderson, Edward A. Geary, Charles S. Peterson, and Ignacio Garcia. I especially value Professor Garcia's comments because he gave me the insights of someone who has experienced Spanish-speaking congregations in the United States. Although we did not always agree, his suggestions helped me improve my arguments. My father listened to me read a draft, my sister Lydia Embry heard my complaints, and my friend Ron Shook celebrated each completed step.

Of course, this monograph would not be possible without the willingness of the interviewees who shared their experiences. Their interviews, preserved by the LDS Church Historical Department and the Charles Redd Center, will continue to be valuable documents as Mormons look at the experiences of Latino American Mormons.

In the end though, the ideas in this monograph are my own. I hope they will be a starting point to help LDS members and others interested in the experiences of Latino Americans look at the fastest growing minority in the United States.

"IN HIS OWN LANGUAGE"

Mormon Spanish Speaking Congregations in the United States

INTRODUCTION

Latino Americans are the fastest growing minority in the United States. According to the 1990 U.S. Census, 19.5 million people of Hispanic origin live in the United States; 61.2 percent are of Mexican origin. Seventeen million speak Spanish at home. Many Latino American scholars point out that figure is probably low. Language difficulties and not wanting to report illegal status in the U.S. are some of the reasons that Hispanics are often underestimated in the census. Scholars estimate that by 2010 there will be more Latinos than African Americans.[1]

Unlike many Northern European American groups who came to the United States in the nineteenth century, Latinos have not abandoned their culture and language. Many continue to speak Spanish. As a result, the U.S., state, and local governments, businesses, and schools cannot assume that immigrants will follow the myth that newcomers would learn English, Americanize, and blend into the "melting pot."

English-speaking Americans have reacted to the increasing Spanish-speaking minority both positively and negatively. Some have demanded that the U.S. Congress pass laws making English the official language, thus avoiding the need to provide resources in other languages, especially Spanish. California passed a law in 1994 denying government assistance to illegal immigrants. Many English-speaking residents of that state felt that Spanish-speaking newcomers were taking over. As Latinos have moved into some California neighborhoods, European Americans have moved out. Americans with these attitudes hold the traditional view, popular since the nineteenth century, that all newcomers should assimilate.

In contrast, some Americans have realized that Latinos are here to stay and that newcomers' needs, including Spanish-language assistance, must be met. Government agencies employ people who speak both Spanish and English. Some fast food restaurants in Southern California hire only bilingual employees. Schools pay teacher assistants who can help Spanish-speaking students and give more attention to multiculturalism. In history classes, for example, teachers talk about the Hispanic tradition in the United States, not just the Anglo American founding fathers.

While English-speaking Americans have focused on these various ways to deal with the Spanish-speaking citizens and aliens, Latinos have resented being lumped together. They may all speak Spanish, but that is often the only similarity. For example, many Argentine ancestors came from Europe, and Argentine Americans have kept European traditions. Some Peruvian Americans also have mainly European roots, lived in large modern cities, and are offended when asked if they had cars and running water in their home country. The converse is also true: Some Peruvian Americans came from rural mountain villages with Indian rather than Spanish traditions; they sometimes lack modern conveniences. Others are blends of European, native, and African backgrounds. Latino scholars believe Northern European Americans need to recognize these long-standing cultural and ethnic differences rather than consider all Spanish-speaking people as the same.

These concerns have also impacted American churches. Traditionally most Latinos have been Catholics. A 1990 National Survey of Religious Identification reported that 65.8 percent of 22 million Hispanic Americans (the number it identified) said they were Catholics. About one-quarter (24.6 percent) were Protestant. Among the other religions listed .8 percent were Mormon. (Another .8 percent refused to answer.)[2]

All these churches face the same dilemmas that governments, schools, and businesses have had to deal with in the United States. How do the religious organizations attract Latinos to their churches? Then how can they best meet the needs of the Spanish-speaking members? Do they encourage the non-English speaking members to attend English services so that they can assimilate into the mainstream? Or do they provide separate congregations with Spanish-language services? And how do they deal with the various cultures represented? Do they put everyone who speaks Spanish together despite their different cultural and ethnic backgrounds?

The Church of Jesus Christ of Latter-day Saints has struggled with these questions and not found an easy solution. This monograph will examine the various approaches the Mormon Church has tried in dealing with Latino Americans and analyze its successes and failures. It will focus on the missions and congregations that the Church has established for Spanish-speaking people in the United States. The topic is timely in Mormon circles as general and local church leaders and all Latter-day Saints meet more Latino American Mormons at church. It can also provide a case study for those interested in how Latinos can fit into American society, especially American-based churches.

I could use many terms to describe the Mormon Church, Spanish-speaking Americans, and English-speaking Americans. Terms that were acceptable in the past are often frowned on now. While the LDS Church has been referred to as the "Mormon Church" for years, leaders have recently discouraged that term because it eliminates the mention of Christ. Yet the complete name of the Church is too long for ease in reading. I use "LDS" and "Mormon."

The preferred name for Spanish-speaking Americans has also changed. In the 1960s the popular term was "Chicano." Later some used "Hispanic Americans." Now "Latino" or "Latino American" is used more often. I will use "Latino," "Latino American," and "Hispanic American," all referring to the same group. Spanish-speaking members of the Church of Jesus Christ of Latter-day Saints are referred to as "Hispanic American Mormons," "LDS Latino Americans," etc. Again, these terms refer to the same group of people. When the person is an immigrant or I know the origin of the person's ancestors, I will refer to him/her as Mexican American, Argentinean American, etc.

Identifying non-Spanish-speaking Americans is equally as difficult. In the past they have been referred to as Anglos or Anglo Americans. Yet they represent the descendants of a wide blend of people other than just English. A common term used in the 1990s is European Americans, yet the Iberian peninsula is also in Europe. Depending on the situation, I will use the terms European American, Anglo American, or English-speaking American. In this monograph they all mean the non-Spanish-speaking population of the United States.

To learn more about how the LDS Church is responding to its Latino American members, the first chapter will look at the sources available on the subject. Chapter two looks at mission work among Latinos in the United States. Chapter three examines the branches created for Spanish-speaking members in the U.S. Chapter four explores the elimination of separate missions during the 1970s and the changing policies toward language branches from 1970 to 1997. Chapter five describes the BYU Charles Redd Center's LDS Hispanic American Oral History Project. Chapters six, seven, and eight report how the Redd Center interviewees feel about ethnic wards and branches. The final chapter presents some of my feelings about language congregations.

Notes

1. Cheryl Ann White, "Factors in the Lives of LDS Church Members that Promote and Inhibit the Acquisition of English as a Second Language" (M.A. thesis, Brigham Young University, 1995), 2; Allan Englekirk and Marguerite Marin, "Mexican Americans," *Gale Encyclopedia of Multicultural America,* Rudolph J. Vecoli, ed. (New York: Gale Research Inc., 1995), 908; William A. Henry III, "Beyond the Melting Pot," *Time,* 9 April 1990, 28–31.

2. Barry A. Kosmin and Seymour P. Lachman, *One Nation under God: Religion in Contemporary American Society* (New York: Harmony Books, 1993), 2, 15, 137.

CHAPTER ONE

SOURCES

Information in this monograph comes from the LDS Church Archives, Brigham Young University's Charles Redd Center for Western Studies LDS Hispanic American Oral History Project, and a BYU Linguistic Department "Distance Learning Project."

LDS Church Archives

Manuscript Histories and Minutes

The LDS Church Archives has mission and local congregation records and oral histories that deal with the experiences of Spanish-speaking Mormons in the United States. Mission and congregational records are often spotty. The completeness and level of detail in the manuscript histories and minutes vary greatly from place to place and from different time periods. There are also gaps when records either were not kept or were not forwarded to Church headquarters. After 1983 the Historical Department collected only annual reports from stakes and missions. Despite these weaknesses, the early manuscript histories provide the best background available on Latino American Mormons.

Oral Histories

In 1972 the LDS Church Historical Department began an oral history project to collect the memories of Church leaders and members. Gordon Irving, who had served a Spanish-speaking mission in Chile, conducted over one hundred interviews with mission presidents, missionaries, and members. While he focused on Latin America, he also interviewed a few Latino Americans and Anglo Americans who had worked with Hispanic Americans. These interviews provide valuable information on Spanish-speaking branches during especially the early 1970s, supplementing the sketchy information in the other Church records.

Charles Redd Center Hispanic American Oral History Project

Background

In 1984 the Charles Redd Center for Western Studies began interviewing ethnic American Mormons about their experiences in the LDS Church. The first project was collecting 226 oral histories of LDS African Americans. These histories were the basis for *Black Saints in a White Church* (Salt Lake City: Signature Books, 1994). Blacks have had a unique experience in the Mormon Church since men were not allowed to take part in the lay priesthood and men and women could not receive temple blessings until 1978.

The Center has also conducted interviews with 19 German-speaking Americans, 61 Native Americans, 94 Hispanic Americans, 51 Polynesian Americans, and 108 Asian Americans. All these groups could participate fully in Mormon Church programs, but each experienced some type of discrimination and prejudice within the Church. While these groups frequently have the same concerns about their membership in the LDS Church, they are different enough that they could not be discussed in one study. Therefore, this study will only focus on Latino American Mormons. Even that is a very broad subject, so rather than explain all segments of Spanish-speaking Americans' experiences in the United States, this monograph will only look at LDS Spanish-speaking congregations in the United States.

The Interviewers

Three interviewers, all native Spanish speakers, conducted most of the ninety-four interviews in the LDS Hispanic American Oral History Project. They were Esmeralda Meraz, a Mexican American from California; Katuska Serrano, an immigrant from Peru living in Provo, Utah; and Andrea Van Wagenen, an Argentine American from California. Meraz and Serrano were Brigham Young University students. Van Wagenen attended the University of Utah but lived in Provo.

Language

For convenience of transcription, most interviews were in English. However, twenty-one—seventeen in the Los Angeles area and four in Provo—were conducted in Spanish. Elizabeth Valdivieso, a young adult who immigrated with her family from Guatemala, exemplified the reasons for conducting interviews in Spanish. After the first question, Valdivieso responded, "In English? Oh, boy. English is very difficult for me. I'm just not that good."[1] After attempting to respond in English for about fifteen minutes, she asked Serrano if she could speak in Spanish.

The Interviewing Instrument

Alan Cherry, an African American Mormon, developed an outline with questions focusing on religious experiences when he started conducting the LDS Afro-American Oral History Project interviews in 1985. Many questions were based on his twenty-year experience as a Mormon. This basic outline was adapted for use in the LDS Hispanic Oral History Project. The interviewers first asked about early life including family, religious, educational, and work experiences. Then since everyone—whether they grew up in the LDS Church or decided to join later—must at some point make a conscious effort to continue as a Mormon, the questions asked about conversion. Other questions dealt with the role of the LDS Church in the person's life. Finally the interviewees talked about their experiences with LDS English-speaking Americans.

Evaluations from the LDS Hispanic American interviewers and others resulted in adding some questions for the LDS Hispanic American Oral History Project. Many Latino American interviewees were immigrants and joined the Church before they came to the United States, so they answered questions about the Church in their native countries. They also talked about the process of coming to the United States and their experiences with Americans in general and with Mormon Americans. And while very few African Americans attended LDS wards and branches with only blacks, many Hispanic American Mormons went to Spanish-speaking units in the United States. So the Hispanic questionnaire also probed their experiences in Spanish-speaking congregations.

Limitations of the Oral History Study

The Redd Center oral history project does not include a representative sample. First, it is impossible to generalize about a whole group of people based on only 94 examples. LDS Church records do not list nationalities, so it is impossible to determine how many Spanish-speaking Mormons live in the United States. In 1993 there were at least 295 U.S. wards and branches where Spanish was the primary language spoken. That number had grown to at least 354 by 1997.

An even greater problem is the sampling method. Since the interviewers were students, they had limited time and mobility; the Redd Center had limited funds for hiring interviewers and sponsoring travel. As a result, fifty-two interviewees lived in Provo, Utah; thirty-four were BYU students. The interviewers also talked to friends and relatives in Southern California. Some informants had lived in other parts of the United States before they moved to Utah so they could compare their experiences. Most interviewees talked about the uniqueness of living in Utah near the Church-owned university and Church headquarters. Yet the same anxieties showed up in all the interviews wherever the informants lived.

The sample is also nonrepresentative in that only one person was not an active member of the LDS Church. Those who no longer attend meetings do not usually maintain close contact with other members, attend BYU, or leave their forwarding address with the local bishop. While sociologists conducting surveys often oversample for inactive members, we did not do that in this interview project. Certainly the interviewees saw difficulties in the Church and had personal challenges, but they had chosen to deal with them within the Church structure.

Coding

A great temptation in doing any research, and especially using oral histories, is to pick the most interesting stories to include in a book. Frequently they are the dramatic conversion experiences, the negative interactions with LDS English-speaking Americans, or stirring testimonies. Writers may then create skewed generalizations based on these unusual examples. To avoid that trap, I hired BYU sociology students to read the interviews, looking for specific information such as where the interviewees were from, how they came in contact with the LDS Church, their views of English-speaking American Mormons, etc. A copy of the forms they used is included as an appendix. While all the interviewers were given the same outline, they did not ask all the questions, so the readers were not able to supply all the information on the coding form.

BYU Distance Learning Project

In 1993 the Linguistics Department at Brigham Young University conducted a "Distance Learning Project" to determine the needs of non-English speaking Latter-day Saints in the United States. BYU researchers selected sites in New York, Texas, California, and Utah. They chose places where there were many ethnic groups. They found several nationalities in the

New York and California samples. A smaller group but still a variety of ethnic members was found in Utah. The Texas group was mainly Mexican American. The researchers handed out surveys in church meetings. They also conducted individual and group interviews. The interviews focused on language concerns, especially at church. A total of 617 members were surveyed; 315 (51.5 percent) were Spanish. Nearly all (302) of the Spanish members filled out the survey in their native language.

Cheryl White and Dena Marie Wright Erickson, BYU graduate students, wrote theses based on the information gathered from these surveys and interviews.[2] The information in this manuscript comes from the White and Erickson studies. Limitations prevented more extensive use of the BYU study. First, the study's focus was to find out the best ways to teach non-English speakers English. Therefore, the questions asked about the function of English in the respondents' lives, not views of native language wards and branches. Second, the study combined Spanish speakers with other groups. Although the Redd Center research shows the concerns of all ethnic groups in the United States are similar, there are differences, and it is difficult to find just the Hispanics in the available results. Third, the study was designed so that the respondents could not be identified by name.

Finally, the BYU study has the same weakness as the Redd Center oral histories. While initially the researchers wanted to survey active and inactive members, they found it impossible to contact inactive members. Most surveys were distributed at church. Therefore, mainly active members took their survey. Despite these limitations, I will occasionally refer to the results of the BYU survey, especially when discussing the role of language in Spanish-speaking congregations.

Summary

All of these sources provide data to study the missions and branches of Latino American Mormons. The chapters that follow will discuss the information gathered from these records.

Notes

1. Elizabeth Valdivieso Oral History, interviewed by Katuska Serrano, 1991, 1, LDS Hispanic American Oral History Project, Charles Redd Center for Western Studies, Manuscript Division, Harold B. Lee Library, Brigham Young University, Provo, Utah.

2. Dena Marie Wright Erickson, "The Relationship Between Non-Native English Speakers' English Proficiency and Their Callings in the LDS Church in the United States" (M.A. thesis, Brigham Young University, 1995); Cheryl Ann White, "Factors in the Lives of LDS Church Members that Promote and Inhibit the Acquisition of English as a Second Language" (M.A. thesis, Brigham Young University, 1995).

CHAPTER TWO

THE CHURCH OF JESUS CHRIST OF LATTER-DAY SAINTS AND ETHNIC MISSIONS IN THE UNITED STATES

Introduction

The available sources show that like other churches, the Church of Jesus Christ of Latter-day Saints has struggled with how to proselyte among, convert, and retain Hispanic members in the United States. It shares proselyting challenges with Protestant churches which have tried to attract Latinos away from the Catholic Church. Once the Latinos join, though, the LDS Church faces new challenges. Like the Catholic Church, it sees itself as universal, serving all the world. Thus the concept of separate churches based on ethnic background while pragmatically appealing is theologically unacceptable—accounting for a jerky record of abrupt policy changes.[1]

There are some differences, though, between congregations in the Catholic and Mormon churches. In contrast to the Catholic Church's large parishes, the Mormon Church creates small congregations (branches and wards) with no more than five hundred members. The community atmosphere in a ward or branch is very important. Although the very existence of ethnic wards and missions depends on which central policy happens to prevail at the moment, the quality of congregational life frequently depends on personalities and shared culture in the local unit, factors which procedure manuals cannot guarantee.

The urgent proselyting mission of the LDS Church has always made nonmembers of all language and cultural groups potential target populations. Policies regarding how to proselyte have changed frequently because no single method has met all the needs of the ethnic members or the Church leadership. This chapter discusses the history of proselyting among Spanish-speaking U.S. residents.

Historical Background

Most missionary efforts in the United States were with English-speaking Americans. Temporary exceptions were Norwegian speakers in Illinois in the early 1840s, German speakers in New York and Pennsylvania in the late 1840s, and Scandinavians and Germans in the Midwest from the 1870s to 1900.[2] More permanent and larger exceptions have been missions created especially for Native Americans and Spanish-speaking Americans.

Proselyting among Hispanic Americans grew out of a preexisting Mormon commitment to convert Native Americans. Only six months after Joseph Smith organized a church in April 1830, he sent missionaries to preach to the Native Americans in Missouri. Although those efforts were not successful, they established a precedent that has been honored ever since. LDS Church leaders focused on native people in North, Central, and South America because of a belief that the Book of Mormon is a religious and social history of ancient (600 B.C.–A.D. 400) inhabitants of the Americas.

Mexican Mission

In 1874 Brigham Young asked Daniel W. Jones, a veteran of the Mexican War who joined the LDS Church after spending the winter of 1850 among the Mormons, and Meliton G. Trejo, a former Spanish Army officer who felt inspired to come to Utah to find the answers to his religious questions and another LDS convert, to translate *Selected Portions from the Book of Mormon*. In 1875 Jones led a group of five missionaries—Anthony W. Ivins, Helaman Pratt, James Z. Stewart, Ammon M. Tenney, and Robert H. Smith—to Mexico. Although only Jones and Tenney spoke Spanish, they held meetings in Chihuahua and mailed their literature to government officials.

Plotino Rhodacanaty, an instructor of Greek in Mexico City, received the material and started a study group. He requested additional information in 1878, and a year later Apostle Moses Thatcher from the Council of Twelve, Trejo, and other Mormon missionaries arrived in Mexico City. They taught, baptized interested people, and organized a congregation in Mexico City. In the next decade, eighteen missionaries served in Mexico, baptizing 241 converts and organizing two branches.

Missionary work ended in June 1889 when the First Presidency, then consisting of Wilford Woodruff, George Q. Cannon, and Joseph F. Smith, closed the mission. Reasons for this action included a general lack of response among urban Mexicans, an expectation among rural Mexicans that they would be subsidized as Protestant missions did, and the deaths of several missionaries and Apostle Abraham O. Woodruff of smallpox. But most important were the financial and political hardships in Utah during the Church's struggle with the federal government over polygamy and political control.[3]

A separate but related Mormon initiative occurred as polygamists fleeing federal prosecution sought refuge in northern Mexico. In 1884 Church President John Taylor wrote Christopher Layton, a polygamist living in Arizona, "Our counsel has been and is to obtain a place of refuge under a foreign government to which our people can flee when menaced in this land." Taylor authorized Apostles George Teasdale and Moses Thatcher, Alexander F. McDonald, president of the Maricopa Stake in Arizona, Layton, and other church members to explore the Mexican states of Sonora and Chihuahua. They purchased land near Casa Grande in Chihuahua, and recruited settlers. By May 1885 about four hundred prospective colonists were ready to enter the country. They established six communities in Chihuahua and two in Sonora. While these towns resembled Utah villages and the residents had limited contact with Mexicans, some learned Spanish and later served in a revitalized Mexican Mission.[4]

Anthony W. Ivins, one of the first missionaries to Mexico and its mission president from 1883 to 1884, returned in 1895 as stake president of the Mormon colonies and as the leader of all Mormons in Mexico. At first he focused on the colonies, but in 1901 he suggested that Church President Lorenzo Snow reopen the Mexican Mission and that Ammon M. Tenney, a 1876 missionary to Mexico, preside. Tenney was already living in the colonies with his families. Tenney, accompanied by Ivins and Apostle John Henry Smith, established mission headquarters in Mexico City in 1901.[5]

Hyrum H. Harris and Talma E. Pomeroy also served as mission presidents during the next six years. In 1907 President Joseph F. Smith called Rey L. Pratt, a former missionary, as president, a position he held until his death twenty-three years later. During that time, Mexican dictator Porfirio Diaz was forced out of office, and revolutionary groups fought for control. To avoid taking sides and to escape the warring factions, American Mormons abandoned the colonies and the Mexican Mission temporarily in 1912–13, with the U.S. government paying evacuation expenses. American Mormon women and children came to the United States by train; the men followed on horse back. Most Mexican missionaries were released so they could return to their families in the colonies. Remaining elders only labored "in the valleys near the conference headquarters where they can work unmolested." The last seven missionaries left the country in September 1913. Rey L. Pratt, still mission president, took up residence in Salt Lake City and corresponded regularly with the Mexican Saints.[6]

While Pratt wanted to return to Mexico, Church President Joseph F. Smith asked him not to go back until the political situation was more stable. Instead in June 1915 Smith asked Pratt to go to Denver, the Western States Mission headquarters, and work with Mexican Americans living in Colorado, New Mexico, Arizona, Texas, and California. Some proselyting had already occurred among the Mexicans in Manassa, Colorado, so Pratt established his headquarters there.[7]

At first, local Mexican Americans served as part-time missionaries. Beginning in August 1915, full-time missionaries were called to work with the Spanish-speakers in the Southwest. Pratt reported, "Opportunities were never better for doing missionary work than at the present time among the Mexicans of the United States, and, judging from the eagerness with which the people receive the elders and the message they bring to them, there is every reason to hope for a mighty harvest of souls in the near future."[8]

He did not overestimate Hispanic interest in the Mormon message. During the winter of 1915–16, elders in Colorado and New Mexico distributed tracts and sold Bibles. One elder sold sixty Bibles in one month. John L. Herrick, president of the Western States Mission, told Pratt that the Spanish-speaking elders had more investigators in three meetings than all of the rest of the Western States Mission combined. By the summer of 1916 the missionaries had baptized nine Mexicans.[9]

Pratt and Herrick recommended to Church President Joseph F. Smith in April 1918 that the Church organize a Spanish-speaking mission. The next month church leaders reestablished the Mexican Mission to work with the Mexican Americans in Arizona, Texas, New Mexico, Colorado, and California. Six months later Pratt moved his headquarters from Manassa to El Paso, Texas, closer to the Mexican population in the United States and to Mexico. In March 1919 he established a Spanish-speaking branch in Mesa, Arizona.[10]

Pratt was delighted with the new efforts. Before leaving Mexico in 1913, he had told Church members the mission would never be completely closed. The mission history reported, "Although there had been many dark days when it seemed that the mission would be abandoned, now he would see the fulfillment of that prophecy." Pratt added in 1919 that the day would come when there would be "not only 25 missionaries but 25,000 missionaries" working with the "people of Israel."[11]

Despite unsettled conditions in Mexico, elders worked both sides of the border. In 1921 the Church again called full-time missionaries to Mexico, while some Spanish-speaking elders and sisters continued to work in the

United States. In 1926 Mexico passed a law allowing only native-born ministers, and the missionaries who were United States citizens left again. The mission was not disbanded but concentrated its energy on the southwest U.S. border.[12]

In 1928 Pratt applauded the efforts of the missionaries, explaining they had organized the Church "across the continent from San Diego, California, to Brownsville, Texas." He acknowledged that it was difficult for the missionaries to "labor . . . in a country where the English language is spoken, but with a call to teach the gospel to a people who speak another tongue." But they had "enjoyed the spirit of the work."[13] The elders and sisters had many potential investigators. Pratt wrote, "In the city of Los Angeles alone it is estimated that there are between fifty and seventy-five thousand Mexican people living in sections of the city pretty much by themselves" so the missionaries had "no difficulty in confining their labors to a people who speak a foreign language." When Apostle Joseph Fielding Smith came to Laredo, Texas, 220 people attended conference sessions. Only a few years before, Pratt had been unable to find anyone interested in the message there.[14] Leland and McNone Perry, a husband and wife who served most of their missions separately during the 1920s, recalled that it was easy to do their Spanish missionary work in Texas since the Mexican Americans lived in one section of town.[15]

After Pratt's death in 1932, a new mission president, Antoine R. Ivins, Anthony W. Ivins's son and a member of the First Quorum of Seventy, continued the Spanish-speaking efforts in the United States. His first year he protested mildly of having in the city of Los Angeles "no less than one hundred and fifty thousand Mexicans" but only "four boys and two young ladies" in the area. He added, however, the limited missionary force was "accomplishing a wonderful work."[16] His 1933 report claimed 4,133 members and thirty eight U.S. Spanish-speaking branches in his mission.[17]

Jurisdictional problems were inevitable since the Mexican Mission covered the same territory as several English-speaking missions. In 1935 Harold W. Pratt, then president of the Mexican Mission, reported that there was potential for Spanish-speaking missionary work in Denver which had 25,000 Mexicans and twenty Mexican American Mormons in the city who were members of the Western States Mission. He felt the Mexicans would be happier in their own branch since some did not speak English and suffered as he delicately put it a "race complex" when working with European Americans. While the Western States Mission president, Joseph J. Daynes, would be willing to organize the branch, Pratt thought he would not "welcome" proselyting missionaries from the Mexican Mission. Pratt reluctantly recommended not assigning missionaries or creating the branch.[18]

Spanish American Mission

In September 1935 Harold Pratt suggested to J. Reuben Clark, a member of the First Presidency and a former U.S. ambassador to Mexico, that the Church divide the Mexican Mission along the international boundary and reopen missionary work in Mexico by calling young men and women who claimed Mexican citizenship. The First Presidency, led by President Heber J. Grant, agreed, creating the Spanish American Mission in April 1936. The Spanish American Mission was headquartered in Los Angeles; the Mexican Mission had its headquarters in Mexico City.[19]

The new Spanish American mission president, Orlando Williams, a deputy sheriff from Mesa, Arizona, moved the mission headquarters to El Paso and energetically urged on the work. In 1938 he reported in General Conference, "We of the Spanish American Mission, like others who are laboring among those who speak Spanish, have a love that is deep for those people." Williams dedicated three chapels for the mission's branches in 1938 and in 1939 recorded as his greatest achievements the completion of chapels and the members staffing the branches.[20]

Other mission presidents were David F. Haymore (1940–43), Lorin F. Jones (1943–53), Harold I. Bowman (1953–58), Ralph E. Brown (1958–61), Melvin R. Brown (1961–64), Donald E. Matthews (1964–67), and Dean L. Larsen (1967). Initially, the mission was very large, covering all the Spanish-speakers in Texas, New Mexico, Colorado, Arizona, and California. Boyd M. Burbidge, a missionary from 1949 to 1951, talked about the size of the mission, lamenting, "Poor President Jones! . . . He worked six months in Texas, New Mexico, and Colorado, and six months in Arizona and California."[21] In 1951 Church President David O. McKay transferred the Spanish work in Colorado, Arizona, and California to stakes and other missions.[22]

In March 1954, Clifford E. Young, a Seventy, toured the mission just after Bowman became president and "praised the superb hospitality of the native members and told of the refinement and culture apparent in their homes, dress and demeanor." He said that despite language difficulties and some opposition, "the mission staff of 68 elders and four local part time missionaries is achieving remarkable success."[23] Bowman recalled that visit, noting that initially Young was concerned about speaking through an interpreter. But by the end of his visit he did not want to talk to Anglos. He said that was like talking to a wall. He liked the way the Spanish people responded, nodding and crying during his talks. That year the mission's manuscript history included reports from thirty branches. Bowman remembered there were 2,330 members.[24]

During his presidency, Bowman made several changes. When he first took over in 1954, he shifted mission headquarters to San Antonio where 60 percent of the residents were Spanish. He also installed members as presidents and leaders in the branches. Members had been staffing only three branches before his presidency and it was a matter of personal pride that when he left missionaries were in charge of only three branches. In 1957 he installed the first Spanish-speaking district presidency in San Antonio. Bowman also established a policy of having branch presidents attend baptismal interviews, adding, "It takes real diplomacy to blend the young missionaries with the older men that preside over the branches."[25]

Bowman lamented that he could not do more to transfer control to the Spanish-speaking members. When Apostle Mark E. Petersen toured the mission, Bowman explained there were enough members for a Spanish-speaking stake but that "the men that handled it [presumably the General Authorities] had no understanding of the people we were handling." An outspoken proponent of ethnic units, he explained that, in mixed congregations "the American . . . is inclined to gobble up the [Mexican], to dominate. . . . But when you give the [Mexicans] the responsibility, it's marvelous how they're able to come forth." Bowman was pleased that when he left the mission in 1958 there were 4,700 members, twelve chapels, and nineteen purchased lots where chapels could be built. There were three branches in San Antonio.[26]

In 1959 General Authority A. Theodore Tuttle toured the mission with the new president, Ralph E. Brown. Tuttle reported, "I was impressed with the humility, sincerity and the dedication of these Spanish-American members," adding that many served in the mission's branches and districts. There were 150 missionaries, 5,000 members, and forty-one branches in the mission. Twelve chapels were under construction with the assistance of labor missionaries.[27]

Two missionaries who served in the late 1940s reported their proselyting experiences in oral histories. Anglo American Sterling Nicolaysen, a missionary from 1946 to 1949, worked as a district president in San Antonio and Denver. He complained that English-speaking Americans discriminated against the Spanish-speaking members. Missionaries were always welcome in English-speaking wards and branches, and Anglo American members attended the Spanish branches' dinners to enjoy the Mexican food; but they did not want the Mexicans to come to district meetings. Sometimes he felt his companions agreed. "I had companions who at the end of the long Sunday wanted to go over to sacrament meeting in the English-speaking branch." Nicolaysen continued this was "a point of conflict" because "I didn't want to go. . . . I was completely satisfied with the work among the Spanish-speaking people."[28]

Nicolaysen also reported that discontinuities occurred because often children of converts who did not speak Spanish did not want to attend church in Spanish units. San Antonio was a unique case where parents stressed Spanish traditions and the young people knew the language. Often first generation Mexicans saw themselves as special because they were Lamanites and insisted on language branches.[29]

Mexican American Samuel Victor Miera, who worked as a missionary from 1948 to 1950, recalled his frustrations when one branch president gave all the sermons and did everything else. "I can't remember anybody else there in that branch." Miera helped run the small branch in Laredo because there were no priesthood members. However, the branch had strong Mutual, Primary, and Relief Society programs.[30]

Like Nicolaysen, Miera saw a clear division between the Spanish and English-speaking branches and missions. The feeling was "you do your work, and we do ours." In Sacramento, California, where there was no language branch, whites "really went out of their way to help us. But in Stockton and Fresno [European Americans] didn't do too much." He concluded that the existence of ethnic branches actually encouraged the English speaking members to feel, "You stay on your side of the track and we stay on ours."[31]

West Spanish American Mission

In 1957 Church leaders surveyed Spanish-speaking members in Colorado, Arizona, and California who had been attending branches assigned to geographical stakes since 1951. They discovered that the stakes had not proselyted among Spanish-speaking Americans because of the language barrier. So the First Presidency under the direction of President David O. McKay organized the West Spanish American Mission on 12 March 1958 and called Leland Perry, who had served in the Mexican Mission in 1925 and was the director of the physical plant at BYU, as president. Grant M. Burbidge replaced Perry, serving as president from 1961 to 1965.[32]

Immediately after forming the mission, Elder Spencer W. Kimball toured the area with Perry, meeting with branch and stake leaders and the general membership. Kimball's message was always the same. First, he explained the Church leaders were creating the mission to more effectively serve the 5 million Spanish Americans in California, Arizona, and Nevada. In most areas, he advised that branches should remain attached to stakes rather than shifting to mission jurisdiction. For example, in Los Angeles, Kimball explained the stake offered a patriarch, the offices of seventies and high priests, and stake meetings. Under mission jurisdiction, the members would lose many of those benefits and could participate only in district conferences. The mission minutes recorded, "Elder Kimball pointed out that he was not trying to sway their thinking, but only to clear up the question. He said that it was his opinion that the mission could never do as much for the branch as the stake can."[33]

Nearly all the members agreed to continue under stake jurisdiction. In Douglas, Arizona, however, most of the thirty Spanish-speaking members were attending a branch in Agua Priesta, Mexico. Five or six were going to the Douglas Ward, but most of the older members were inactive because of language and transportation problems. If the mission formed a branch, leadership would have to come from the ward, and the local leaders did not want the responsibility. So Kimball decided that the Spanish-speaking members should continue to attend the Agua Priesta Branch, which would be part of the Northern Mexican Mission. But Kimball pleaded with the English-speaking American members: "Tolerance is not enough; we must accept our brothers and sisters, the children of Adam, in full fellowship. We should sing together and pray together." Kimball also asked the ward to provide classes for those who did not speak English.[34]

Since the branches remained parts of stakes, Perry was relieved of the responsibilities of supervising branches, working with members, maintaining their records, and collecting their tithing. He supported the concept of separate Spanish branches because he felt that the people should learn about the Church in their own language and that most Hispanics were "quiet and forgotten" in integrated wards. However, he explained a branch in a geographical stake worked well. In most cases, a member of the high council who spoke Spanish worked with the branch. Most branch presidents were Anglo American, but the counselors were usually Mexicans. Branch members were well versed in the scriptures and had good knowledge of the gospel. Finding a place to meet was sometimes challenging, but most of the branches had their own chapels.[35]

To better understand the Spanish-speaking people in California and Arizona, Perry assigned a missionary couple, Roland G. and Elizabeth E. Kaiser, to survey the mission area in 1958. The Kaisers visited the missionaries and local branches and conducted research with government and business leaders to learn how many and where Spanish-speaking people lived. Perry forwarded these reports, updated in 1961, to the First Presidency.[36]

Despite the problems of illegal immigration, which made exact figures problematic, the Kaisers estimated that California had 1,011,200 Spanish-speaking residents and Arizona had 171,440. Nearly 60 percent of those in California (600,000) lived in the Los Angeles area. The next highest concentration was the San Francisco Bay Area (126,416). An estimated 78 percent were native-born U.S. citizens, 6 percent were naturalized citizens, and 16 percent were aliens. According to their records, 183,000 Mexicans entered the United States between July 1955 and July 1956—about 500 a day. Some Spanish speakers maintained their language into the third generation, 38 percent spoke only Spanish, 20 percent spoke only English, and 42 percent spoke both languages.[37]

Spanish speakers lived throughout the cities rather than in ethnic neighborhoods and many English-speaking Hispanics wanted to talk in that language. As a result, West Spanish American missionaries did 20 to 30 percent of their work in Spanish. In those cities where there were Spanish "colonies," African Americans were moving into that section of town, and, according to the Kaisers, the Spanish population was "being diluted at an alarming rate."[38]

Additional barriers faced Spanish-speaking converts. Sometimes they had to travel long distances to a Spanish branch. Church buildings were often inadequate. The San Diego Branch was "poorly housed, poorly staffed, poorly attended, and inconveniently located." The Fresno Branch was in a "dilapidated cement block hall which is entirely inadequate and a disgrace to the Church." In 1961 after the city condemned the property, the branch rented a different building. Discrimination was real from European American members. The Kaisers wrote, "The thinking and attitude of stake, ward and branch officials toward these people need to be changed. We have a race barrier whether we like it or not."[39]

Other Missionary Efforts Among Latino Americans, 1960s

In 1964 during the New York World's Fair, elders came from the Spanish American Mission to work at the Mormon pavilion. Several Redd Center

Latino American interviewees visited that exhibit. Roberto Ayerdis, originally from Honduras, was twelve years old at the time of the fair. He recalled that his parents had joined the Church but become inactive. When his father took him to the World's Fair, "smack in the middle of the world's fair the Church had a pavilion." He continued, "There was a concentration of Lamanites in New York by that time, so there was a big concentration of Spanish-speaking missionaries that were expressly sent to the World's Fair. So we got re-acquainted with the Church." As a result, the Ayerdis family returned to the LDS Church.[40]

Myriam Lopez Furrows, a native of Puerto Rico, was nine years old in 1964. Her sister went to the fair and filled out a referral card at the Mormon exhibit. That sister was never around when the missionaries came, but Myriam, a seventeen-year-old sister, and her two brothers—ages eleven and thirteen—listened to the discussions and decided to join. Their father refused to let them be baptized on Christmas morning, but he agreed to let them on New Year's Eve.[41]

As a result of the fair, many Spanish-speaking people on the East Coast requested more information. Church leaders sent Spanish-speaking missionaries to the Eastern States, Delaware-Maryland, and Florida missions. In 1971 missionaries in the eastern U.S. were working with new immigrants from throughout Latin America. In November 1966 the Spanish American Branch was organized as part of the New York Stake. In 1977 it became a ward.[42]

Salt Lake Valley Regional Mission

Background

While there were only four—two Native American and two Spanish-speaking—missions designed to work exclusively with ethnic groups in the United States, there was a precedent of congregations, social groups, and newspapers for other ethnic groups. During the nineteenth century, Welsh-, German-, and Danish-speaking Saints had their own meetings in Salt Lake City, often visited by General Authorities.[43]

Although these congregations were purportedly temporary—transitional structures while newcomers learned English and adjusted to geographical wards—Church leaders simultaneously encouraged the members to continue to use their native languages and to teach them to their children as preparation for missions. With this tacit encouragement, some of the language branches proved long-lived and more developed. In 1923 a Committee on Latter-day Saints Meetings and Newspapers in Foreign Languages chaired by Apostle John A. Widstoe conducted a survey and found thirty "foreign" units serving 3,014 members in twenty-one stakes. Four were for "Mexicans." The other twenty-six units were for Northern European languages.[44]

In the 1920s the U.S. Congress passed laws restricting immigration. LDS Church leaders also stopped encouraging members to gather to Zion. Many new members stopped trying to come as well since there were no longer economic incentives. As the older immigrants died off and the new generation became fluent in English, there was less need for non-English meetings and newspapers. All of the Church newspapers were discontinued in 1935.[45]

During World War II, anti-foreigner sentiments were high in the United States. As a result, the First Presidency discontinued all foreign-language activities in the Salt Lake Valley except the Mexican Branch "for the duration of the war, or until further instruction from the First Presidency."[46] While there are no records showing Church leaders' motives, the feeling of many German-speaking American Mormons was that many Americans and especially the government were uncomfortable with German meetings being held while the U.S. was at war.

Organization of a Regional Mission

After World War II, an influx of new immigrants from Europe and other areas prompted not only a revival of ethnic congregations in the Salt Lake Valley but also formal missionary efforts among regional ethnic groups. Regional missions, as they were called, were established in 1952 in the Salt Lake Valley, Ogden, the Uintah Basin, and Pocatello, Idaho.[47]

Elder Kimball was enthusiastic about these new missions. At the general Relief Society conference in 1952, he urged the women to be involved in the proselyting efforts in the Salt Lake Valley. "We have far more Lamanite people speaking the Spanish language in the stakes of Zion. . . . It is far easier for us to teach the Gospel to the Japanese, the Chinese, Italians, Greeks, and Spanish here than to go to their homelands where laws and competition . . . limit our efforts." He also made an important distinction between Mormon culture and the gospel, explaining that they did not need to learn to quilt. "Instead, our goal is to make gods of the Lamanite people and the other minority people. It is to build character, it is to build faith, it is to give them knowledge of their Lord and His program."[48]

Anglo American Ralph Williams Evans, a former president of the Southwest Indian Mission, became the first president of the Salt Lake Regional Mission. He chose two Anglo Americans, G. Wallace Fox and Arval L. Steadbeck, as counselors. The mission worked directly with the twenty-seven stakes in the Salt Lake Valley. Stake presidents selected missionaries, often men and women who had served on foreign missions and learned another language. The leaders then estimated that there were about 5,000 non-English-speaking Mormons in 1,483 families, with Mexicans comprising 22 percent of the total (1,144).[49]

Succeeding Evans in 1956 was L. Sidney Shreeve, the executive director of the Utah Society for Crippled Children and Adults. Shreeve had served an LDS mission to Argentina from 1936 to 1938 and as president of the Spanish-speaking branch in Mesa, Arizona. He chose as counselors Ray Pawiki, a Hopi, and Gerald Okabe, a Japanese Hawaiian. Missionaries taught in Spanish, Navajo, Japanese, German, Dutch, Portuguese, French, Norwegian, and Italian and enjoyed particular success among the Spanish Americans and Japanese Americans. Shreeve later described it as "very exciting work. . . . We had a regular little United Nations, only we operated in harmony and toward one common goal—the building of the Lord's Kingdom here on earth."[50]

Anglo American Golden Buchanan, the third president of the mission (1959–66), was originally from Richfield, Utah, where he was instrumental in starting the Indian Placement Program. During the 1950s he also presided over the Southwest Indian Mission and served as the Church's coordinator of Indian Affairs. He described himself initially as an integrationist: People who understood English should be in an English ward. But after working with the minority groups, he changed his stance, realizing the benefits members felt in worshiping with others of their own nationality. One reason he admitted was there was not enough fellowshipping in the geographical wards.[51]

Ethnic Branches

An outgrowth of the mission's effort was the organization of foreign language Sunday Schools during the 1950s which led in turn to the reestablishment in 1962 and 1963 of Japanese, German, Dutch, Swedish, Danish, two Spanish (Cumorah and Helaman), and two Native American branches. French, Mandarin, and Cantonese Sunday Schools were also organized.[52]

Spencer W. Kimball, along with Mark E. Petersen, organized many of these ethnic branches. Afterwards, Kimball visited these congregations whenever he did not have assignments out of town. He was always pleased with their activities. On 14 July 1963 he wrote in his journal that he attended the Swedish, Norwegian, and Dutch meetings and spoke through interpreters. He recalled, "These are branches that I helped to organize several months ago, and I feel very happy in their accomplishments and the strength of these new units. It serves a very important purpose to give to the language groups or those not understanding English, a chance to worship here in Salt Lake in their own tongue and they are deeply appreciative of it." He observed that the branches served mainly adults since the children spoke English.[53]

In 1967 Kimball attended a conference for all the minority branches, proudly reporting that people speaking twenty languages were there, including four or five Native American languages. The branches were having remarkable success: 90 percent home teaching, 85 percent attendance at sacrament, 69 percent attendance at priesthood, 68 percent at Sunday School, and 62 percent at Relief Society. In addition, there had been forty-two baptisms and thirty-three reactivations.[54]

Lyman Shreeve also strongly supported the branches. While the ultimate goal was always integration "after they were well indoctrinated in Church principles and firm in the faith," new converts or recently reactivated ethnic members needed "a little group that we could control and work with." Minority members, often left out in the geographical wards, could "blossom" in the ethnic branches.[55] During the 1960s all but the Chinese fully staffed their own congregations without the assistance of English-speaking members. The German branch averaged 125 to 150 percent attendance and the Japanese branch also attracted members and visitors.[56]

With the widespread establishment of ethnic branches during the 1960s, the ethnic members had religious homes. Attached to geographical stakes, many ethnic branches in the area continue to operate in 1997.[57]

Programs

While missionaries taught in many languages, many Church programs and curriculum materials sometimes lagged. As part of the opening of the Mexican Mission, the Church published the Book of Mormon in Spanish in 1886.[58] In 1928 Mission President Rey L. Pratt did another translation of the Book of Mormon. He also translated missionary pamphlets such as *A Friendly Discussion* and *Is Baptism Essential for Salvation* and wrote others in Spanish to help in the missionary work. In 1939 Eduardo Balderas was asked to come to Salt Lake City from El Paso, Texas, where he worked with other Spanish translators on books such as James E. Talmage's *Jesus the Christ*.[59]

Temple Work

Mormons believe that temple ordinances are essential for salvation, but for a century these ceremonies were only in English.[60] The first translation authorized by Church President Heber J. Grant was in Spanish. In 1944 Antoine Ivins was asked to direct the work and asked Balderas to help him. When it was completed, it was available only at the Arizona Temple.[61] Lyman Shreeve, who served as president of the Spanish-speaking Mesa Branch, recalls attending the Arizona Temple before 1943 with Spanish-speaking members and providing a whispered translation during the ceremony.[62]

From 1945 to 1967, the Church sponsored an annual "Lamanite Conference" in Mesa at which Spanish-speaking members from the United States and Mexico attended the temple and received instructions from Church leaders. (Despite the conferences' name, Native Americans such as nearby Navajos apparently were not invited unless they spoke Spanish.) Balderas recalled the first conference, "Of course that first excursion was a wonderful, historical occasion. It was an conference and an excursion at that time."[63] At the third meeting in 1948 Spencer W. Kimball described the future of the Spanish-speaking people. "I see the Lamanites coming into this Church. Instead of coming in small groups of tens or hundreds, they will be in thousands. I see them organized into wards and stakes with Lamanite people comprising these stakes. I see them filling temples and officiating therein."[64]

The next year David O. McKay, an apostle, welcomed 341 Spanish-speaking members from twenty-six branches in the Mexican and Spanish American missions and from four stakes outside the missions. In 1953 Lorin F. Jones, the outgoing Spanish American Mission president, spoke to the 300 Mexicans and Mexican Americans attending the conference. Two years later by then President David O. McKay again addressed the group, telling those present: "Because of your faithfulness and diligence, . . . we were impressed to give other people the opportunity of receiving these blessings in their own language."[65]

These conferences grew in popularity. When Apostle Mark E. Petersen spoke in 1958, the *Church News* reported that nearly 1,000 Spanish-speaking Saints from the United States and Mexico gathered to attend the temple and other meetings, many coming at great sacrifice. The next year Elder Kimball spoke to 800 members. Increasing attendance and the expansion of the Church in Latin America prompted the addition in 1966 of other sessions: one was added in the spring and three in the fall. Large groups from Latin America, Texas, Arizona, and California stakes, plus individual Spanish-speaking members from California, Utah, and New Mexico, swelled the ranks of temple attendance.[66]

In 1967 the Arizona Temple scheduled regular Spanish sessions on the first and third Friday of each month. In 1973, when Balderas was interviewed, the Arizona, Los Angeles, and Oakland temples were showing an endowment film in Spanish and the Provo Temple was just starting to show the film.[67] Eventually all but the Manti and Salt Lake temples showed films so the temple ceremonies were available via headsets in all languages in nearly all temples.

Relief Society

In 1956 the Relief Society general presidency, Belle S. Spafford, Marianne C. Sharp, and Velma N. Simmonsen, arranged to translate lessons into Spanish. These lessons were not always the same as those taught in English-speaking units. The first year the theology and visiting teaching messages were the lessons that had been taught in English the year before (1954–55). The Spanish literature and social science courses in 1956 came from books by Joseph Fielding Smith. In "Notes to the Field," Relief Society leaders encouraged European American leaders in "minority" branches to choose lessons that fit their sisters' needs.[68]

Beginning in 1966, the First Presidency and Council of Twelve authorized the translation of the entire *Relief Society Magazine* with its fiction, reports of Relief Society General Conferences, and weekly lessons. In an article announcing the decision, Apostle Marion G. Romney explained, "Today, the Spanish-speaking Relief Society members constitute the greatest number next to the English-speaking members." He continued, "Personally, I am very grateful that, after these many years, the Spanish-speaking sisters may now have access to the same material and inspiration as do the sisters near the headquarters of the Church." The Mercedes Branch in the San Antonio area called the translation a "great blessing."

They had enjoyed having the lessons but now they were glad to have the complete program.[69]

In October 1963 Kimball recorded in his journal that he explained the Relief Society programs for Spanish-speaking and Native Americans to Church President McKay. McKay agreed all auxiliaries should provide the special programs.[70]

Magazines and Lesson Manuals

However, except for the *Relief Society Magazine*, none of the other auxiliary magazines appeared in Spanish. When Balderas started translating for the Church in 1939, the translation department worked on Spanish manuals for other organizations such as the Sunday School or Mutual Improvement Associations. This continued during World War II and the years following. However, it was impossible to translate all the manuals for all classes and they were frequently given to the Spanish-speaking members a year after they were used in English-speaking wards and branches.[71]

In 1944 *Liahona: An Elders' Journal*, a journal for missionaries published in Independence, Missouri, was eliminated. A new journal by the same name was published in Spanish out of Mexico City from 1944 to 1955. Then in 1967 new magazines designed for non-English speaking members were announced for nine languages. The magazine consisted primarily of articles from the English magazines with a local news insert. The title, which varied by language, continued to be *Liahona* for the Spanish speakers. That same year eight television stations in Mexico carried general conference in Spanish, Church employees translated LDS hymns, and the Church announced members would receive the lesson manuals, in many languages, including Spanish, simultaneously as part of the correlation effort.[72]

The *Relief Society Magazine* was published in English and Spanish until the First Presidency and Quorum of the Twelve consolidated the English magazines in 1970. The *Improvement Era*, *Relief Society Magazine*, and Sunday School *Instructor* became one adult English magazine, the *Ensign*. The *New Era* replaced a small section in the *Improvement Era* and became a teenage magazine, and the *Friend* was for children ages three to twelve.[73]

Summary

Over the years, the Mexican, Spanish American, West Spanish American, and Salt Lake Regional missions all worked with Spanish-speaking

Americans in the United States. Through these missions and other programs, the LDS General Authorities attempted to proselyte among Latino Americans and meet the needs of the new members. The general Church also established programs for Spanish-speaking members in the United States and throughout the world. An important part of the effort to serve Hispanic Americans was also the establishment of Spanish-speaking congregations, the subject of the next chapter.

Notes

1. There are many books that discuss the relationships of various churches with Latino American Mormons. However, attempts to summarize them for this study proved to be too sketchy and incomplete. Those interested in other churches' responses to Spanish-speaking Americans will find the following sources helpful. Barry A. Kosmin and Seymour P. Lachman, *One Nation under God: Religion in Contemporary American Society* (New York: Harmony Books, 1993); Clifton L. Holland, *The Religious Dimension in Hispanic Los Angeles, a Protestant Case Study* (South Pasadena, CA: William Carey Library, 1974); Randi Jones Walker, *Protestant in the Sangre de Cristos, 1850–1920* (Albuquerque: University of New Mexico, 1991); Carlos E. Cortes, *Protestant and Latinos in the United States* (New York: Arno Press, 1980); Kyle Haselden, *Death of a Myth: New Locus for Spanish American Faith* (New York: Friendship Press, 1964); Jay P. Dolan and Allan Figueroa Deck, eds., *Hispanic Catholic Culture in the U.S.: Issues and Concerns* (Notre Dame: University of Notre Dame, 1994); Vicente V. Mayer, "After Escalante: The Spanish-speaking People of Utah," *The People of Utah,* Helen Z. Papanikolas, ed (Salt Lake City: Utah State Historical Society, 1976); Jay P. Dolan, *The American Catholic Experience: A History from Colonial Times to the Present* (Garden City, NY: Doubleday and Company, 1985); Dolores Liptak, *Immigrants and Their Church* (New York: Macmillian, 1989); Jay P. Dolan and Gilberto M. Hinojosa, *Mexican Americans and the Catholic Church, 1900–1965* (Notre Dame: University of Notre Dame Press, 1994); Manuel P. Sarvin, *The Mexican Americans: An Awakening Minority* (Beverly Hills: Glencoe Press, 1970); Isidro Lucas, *The Browning of America: The Hispanic Revolution in the American Church* (Chicago: Fides/Claretian, 1981); Juliana Boerio-Goates, "The Catholic Church and Ethnic Diversity: A Historical and Personal Perspective," *"For ye are all one in Christ Jesus:" The Global Church in a World of Ethnic Diversity* (Provo, UT: David M. Kennedy Center for International Studies, Brigham Young University, 1996).

2. Richard L. Jensen, "Mother Tongue: Use of Non-English Languages in the Church of Jesus Christ of Latter-day Saints in the United States, 1850–1983," *New Views of Mormon History: A Collection of Essays in Honor of Leonard J. Arrington,* Davis Bitton and Maureen Ursenbach Beecher, eds. (Salt Lake City: University of Utah Press, 1987), 274.

3. Gerry R. Flake, "Mormons in Mexico, the First 96 Years," *Ensign* 2 (September 1972):20; Antoine R. Ivins, "Mexican Saints Remain Loyal to the Truth," *Liahona, the Elders' Journal*, 26 April 1932, 544; Rey L. Pratt, "Review of the Missionary Labors Among the Lamanites," *Liahona, the Elders' Journal*, 7 November 1916, 293–94; F. LaMond Tullis, *Mormons in Mexico: The Dynamics of Faith and Culture* (Logan: Utah State University Press, 1987), 17–18, 69–70.

4. Jessie L. Embry, *Mormon Polygamous Families: Life in the Principle* (Salt Lake City: University of Utah Press, 1987), 22–24.

5. Tullis, *Mormons in Mexico*, 73–74.

6. Flake, "Mormons in Mexico," 20; Mexican Mission, Manuscript History, 5 August 1912, 12 August 1912, 21 October 1912, 6 May 1912, 29 August 1913, 16 September 1913, 17 October 1913, LDS Church Archives, Historical Department, Church of Jesus Christ of Latter-day Saints, Salt Lake City, Utah. (Hereinafter cited as LDS Church Archives.)

7. Pratt, "Review," 296.

8. Ibid.

9. Ibid., 295–296.

10. Mexican Mission, Manuscript History, 6 April 1918, 13 April 1918, 17 April 1918, 19 May 1918, 14 November 1918, 13 February 1919, 12 March 1919.

11. Ibid., 2 November 1919.

12. Ibid., 3 November 1919, 27 February 1921, 31 December 1929, history at the beginning of volume 4.

13. Rey L. Pratt, "The Mexican Mission," *Improvement Era* 31 (May 1928): 579–580.

14. Rey L. Pratt, "Religious Conditions in Mexico," *Liahona, the Elders' Journal*, 12 January 1928, 345–346.

15. Leland and McNone Perry, Oral History, interviewed by Gordon Irving, 1972, 9, LDS Church Archives.

16. Antoine R. Ivins, "Mexican Saints," 544.

17. Antoine R. Ivins, "The Mexican Mission," *Improvement Era* 36 (July 1933): 540.

18. Mexican Mission, Manuscript History, 4 June 1935.

19. Ibid., 17 September 1935, 8 October 1935, 22 April 1936, 6 May 1936.

20. Spanish American Mission, Manuscript History, 28 June 1936, September 1936, 4 March 1938, December 1939, September 1940, LDS Church Archives; Orlando C. Williams, Conference Report, *Liahona, the Elders' Journal*, 13 September 1938, 146.

21. Boyd M. Burbidge, Oral History, interviewed by Marcie Goodman, 1992, 1–2, LDS Missionary Oral History Project, Charles Redd Center for Western

Studies, Manuscript Division, Harold B. Lee Library, Brigham Young University, Provo, Utah.

22. Lorin Jones, "Spanish American Mission Reduced in Size," Ivie Jones Papers, LDS Church Archives.

23. Spanish American Mission, Manuscript History, 27 March 1954.

24. Ibid., 31 December 1954; Harold Israel Bowman, Oral History, interviewed by Gordon Irving, 1973, 49–50, 65, LDS Church Archives.

25. Bowman, Oral History, 32–33, 48, 75; "Spanish-Speaking District Presidency Gets Assignment," *Church News*, 23 March 1957, 15; Spanish American Mission, 16 January 1954; 19 March 1954.

26. Bowman, Oral History, 33, 40, 65, 68.

27. "Elder Tuttle Reports Work Among Lamanites," *Church News*, 14 March 1959, 6; "Along the Rio Grande: The Spanish American Mission," *Church News*, 23 April 1960, 12.

28. Sterling Nicolaysen, Oral History, interviewed by William G. Hartley, 1973, 20–21, LDS Church Archives.

29. Ibid.

30. Samuel Victor Miera, Oral History, interviewed by Gordon Irving, 1975–76, 28, 42, LDS Church Archives.

31. Ibid., 29.

32. Perry, Oral History, 46-49; Grant M. Burbidge, Oral History, interviewed by Gordon Irving, 1973, 35, LDS Church Archives.

33. West Spanish American Mission, Manuscript History, 12 March 1958, LDS Church Archives.

34. Ibid.

35. Perry, Oral History, 56-58

36. [Roland G. and Elizabeth E. Kaiser], "Population Survey Pertaining to Spanish-speaking People in California and Arizona, 1958–1961," Los Angeles, 1961, Special Collections, Harold B. Lee Library, Brigham Young University, Provo, Utah.

37. Ibid., 2–4.

38. Ibid., 4–5.

39. Ibid., 6, 10–11; Appendix, 2.

40. Roberto Ayerdis, Oral History, interviewed by Janean Baker, 1992, 11, LDS Hispanic American Oral History Project, Charles Redd Center for Western Studies, Manuscript Division, Harold B. Lee Library, Brigham Young University, Provo, Utah. (Hereinafter referred as LDS Hispanic American.)

41. Myriam Lopez Furrows, Oral History, interviewed by Katuska Serrano, 1991, 8, LDS Hispanic American.

42. "'Spanish' Elders Used in East U.S.," *Church News*, 30 January 1971, 4, 15; New York Spanish American Ward, Manuscript History, 1966–77, LDS Church Archives.

43. Jensen, "Mother Tongue," 276–77.

44. Ibid., 278–80.

45. Ibid., 281.

46. Ibid., 281.

47. Ibid., 287.

48. "Praise Given Women for Mission Work," *Church News*, 4 October 1952, 6.

49. S. Perry Lee, "Salt Lake Valley Mission Created," ibid., 27 September 1952, 3.

50. Lyman Sidney and Afton K. Shreeve, Oral History, interviewed by Gordon Irving, 1974–75, 177–78, LDS Church Archives.

51. Golden Buchanan, Oral History, interviewed by William G. Hartley, 1975, 5:7–8, 65, 73, 118, LDS Church Archives.

52. *Church News*, 21 April 1962, 7; 28 April 1962, 11; Jensen, "Mother Tongue," 287–88.

53. Spencer W. Kimball Journal, 14 July 1963, in private possession. Used by permission of the family.

54. Ibid., 22 February 1967.

55. Shreeve, Oral History, 180–81.

56. Buchanan, Oral History, 1975, 5:138–39.

57. Jensen, "Mother Tongue," 288.

58. "'Word' Rolls out in Many Tongues," *Church News*, 27 February 1971, 5.

59. Eduardo Balderas Oral History, interviewed by Gordon Irving, 1973, 9, 41–42, 58, LDS Church Archives.

60. Indians were endowed in the 1870s and 1880s, and Hawaiian immigrants attended dedication of the Salt Lake Temple in 1893, but there is no record of translators. Jensen, "Mother Tongue," 294.

61. Ibid., 294; Balderas, Oral History, 66.

62. Shreeve, Oral History, 180.

63. Balderas, Oral History, 67.

64. Spanish American Mission, Manuscript History, 15 November 1947 (*Church News* article).

65. Ibid., 10 November 1948, 19 October 1953; Preston R. Nibley, "The Spanish-American Mission," *Relief Society Magazine* 44 (November 1957): 728–29.

66. "Lamanites Make Annual Mesa Temple Excursion," *Church News*, 15 November 1958, 10; Kimball Journal, October 1959; *Church News*, 7 May 1966, 4.

67. *Church News*, 14 January 1967, 12; Balderas, Oral History, 67.

68. "Lesson Work for Spanish-Speaking Relief Societies and Other Minority Groups in Stakes," "Notes to the Field," *Relief Society Magazine* 43 (January 1956): 34.

69. Marion G. Romney, "Relief Society Magazine in Spanish," *Relief Society Magazine* 53 (June 1966): 406–407; Mercedes Branch, Manuscript History, 30 September 1966, LDS Church Archives.

70. Kimball Journal, 11 October 1963.

71. Balderas, Oral History, 42.

72. "Language for non-English Members," *Church News*, 25 March 1967, 3; "Unto Every Nation, Kindred, and Tongue," ibid., 15 April 1967, 3; "Songs of Zion in 11 Languages," ibid., 24 June 1967, 9; "Church Programs in Many Tongues," ibid., 23 September 1967, 6–7.

73. Ibid., 6 June 1970, 8.

CHAPTER THREE

BRANCH HISTORIES

Introduction

Hispanic branches and wards, a logical outgrowth of ethnic proselyting and ethnic Sunday Schools, have played an important role in the lives of Spanish-speaking members in the United States. Whether as parts of missions or stakes, they have provided culturally comfortable places for members to worship in their native language. Yet they also represented a conflict between the pragmatics of proselyting and the theological importance of inclusiveness.

Apostle Spencer W. Kimball was an enthusiastic supporter of ethnic units during his apostolic career largely for utilitarian reasons. For example, in 1963 he met with the stake presidencies in the Phoenix and Mesa area and recorded in his journal, "In the valley they are doing a splendid work and we have several wards and branches for the Mexicans." During the same visit, Kimball also met with Spanish-speaking groups at Buckeye and Tolleson. He noted that forty-one people attended the Buckeye Branch: "It was a very fine little group and they look like they might be solid, firm, new members." The Tolleson Branch had 124 members. He recorded, "I held a good meeting there and was pleased with the attitude and the character of the people."[1]

Kimball also spoke in favor of other ethnic congregations. For example, when he spoke at the organization of the Salt Lake Valley German speaking ward in 1963, he told the members it was "not right" to force everyone to learn English. But at the same meeting, he added that the General Authorities hoped the immigrants would learn English and return to geographical wards.[2]

While Kimball supported the idea of temporary ethnic congregations, other General Authorities disagreed and supported integrated wards in the United States. The debate has continued over the years. For example, in 1988 Quorum of Seventy member Paul H. Dunn spoke in favor of unity: "Do you think when we get to the other side of the veil the Lord is going to care whether you came from Tonga or New Zealand or Germany or

America? . . . No. That's why we call each other brothers and sisters. . . . The color of skin, the culture we represent, the interests we have are all quite secondary to the concept of the eternal family."[3] Yet in 1992 John H. Groberg, a member of the Seventies, explained, "Our prime role . . . is not to teach people English or how to become American. Gospel principles . . . don't vary from language to language. We declare Christ, not English, our mission is not limited to culture."[4]

What has this meant to Latino American Mormons? One way to better understand their experiences is to look at the histories of individual congregations. This chapter will examine selected Spanish-speaking wards and branches.

Salt Lake City

Mexican Branch/Lucero Ward

The Mexican Branch/Lucero Ward is the longest continually operating ethnic unit in the Salt Lake Valley and possibly the United States. The branch traces its history to 1919 and 1920 when the Rivera sisters, Agustina R. Torres, Dolores R. Torres, and Domitila R. Martinez, came to Salt Lake City. They had been active in the Church in Mexico, and they came to Utah to be in Zion. They married and converted their husbands. According to the *Church News,* "They became the nucleus of the Mexican branch which was organized under direction of . . . Elder Melvin J. Ballard of the Council of Twelve" in 1925.[5]

Anthony W. Ivins, who was the stake president in the Mormon colonies and a member of the Twelve and the First Presidency, was also an important influence in starting the Mexican branch. According to James Vernon Sharp, who served in the Mexican Mission from 1924 to 1926 and then worked with the branch first as a counselor (1927–30) when he was twenty-two years old and then as branch president (1933–36), "Ivins had a soft spot in his heart for the Mexican people, and realizing that they were pretty much lost as they went into other areas, it was under his direction that the Mexican Branch was formed."[6]

At first the group met in a local Mexican American's store. Then it met in the Salt Lake Sixth Ward Chapel, and in 1939 began meeting in the Pioneer Stake Hall. The first branch president was Anglo American Horace H. Cummings. The branch presidents who followed were also Anglo Americans: S. Marsena Foster (1927–33), James Vernon Sharp (1933–36),

C. Vernon Jackson (1936–37), James Vernon Graves (1938–41), Vaughn Green (1942–47). Don H. Smith (1947–52), W. Ernest Young (1952–56), Arthur M. Jensen (1956–58), Russell H. Bishop (1958), and Robert Henry Burton (1958–66).[7]

Having Anglo American leaders sometimes created problems. James Vernon Sharp recalled that Apostles Melvin J. Ballard and Harold B. Lee attended the meeting when he was called to be branch president in 1933. His counselors, Anglo Americans who were not members of the branch, had also served Spanish-speaking missions. The secretary, Manuel Torres, was a Hispanic member of the branch.

When Sharp's name was presented, Sharp recalled, "Marguarito Bautista and some others voted against me." Lee, who was conducting, asked Ballard what to do. Ballard then asked why the members had voted against Sharp. Sharp continued, "The folks said they had no complaints against me; they liked me and what I did, but they thought it was time for a Mexican to run the Mexican Branch." Ballard replied that Church leaders had considered calling a Mexican, but "under the direction of the Lord they had been directed to do this and unless they had something derogatory against me, they couldn't entertain that as an excuse." As a result, Sharp was sustained and had "the support of those people while I was there."[8] Sharp continued as branch president for about five years. During that time, he was a student at the University of Utah and part owner of Sharp Electric.

The branch membership grew gradually over the years. In 1928 there were sixty-nine members; two years later there were ninety-two. In 1938, 118 Latinos belonged to the branch. In 1951 the branch moved into its own building at 232 West 800 South. J. Reuben Clark, a member of the First Presidency, dedicated the new building and told the members, "The Lord will expect you to convert your own—you must bring your own to a knowledge of the gospel." At that time Anglo American Don H. Smith was branch president; his second counselor, Homer L. Proctor, was also Anglo American. Mexican American Eduardo Balderas, of the Church's translation department, was the first counselor. The chapel held 130, and an additional 200 could be accommodated in the recreation hall.[9]

Anglo American Robert Henry Burton, who served in the Spanish American Mission in 1938, became president of the Mexican branch in 1958. The next year the branch became the Lucero Ward, and Burton became the first bishop. According to Burton, Apostle Kimball invited him to lunch, asked for names of people who could lead the branch, then called him to the position. Burton chose as counselors Latino Americans

Manuel Torres, one of the oldest members of the branch, and Orlando Rivera, a returned missionary from Colorado who was working on a master's degree in education at the University of Utah. According to the manuscript history, this was a highlight in the branch: "A much awaited event transpired this date. The Salt Lake Mexican Branch was reorganized into a full fledged ward." Apostle Joseph Fielding Smith conducted the meeting. Since all the members were no longer from Mexico, the ward was named Lucero, meaning Star of the Morning. Lucero was also Rey L. Pratt's middle name, and the ward's name also honored him.[10]

Burton recalled his years as branch president and bishop: "With all my shortcomings I always felt I was given good support by the people and made to feel as one of them. . . . Typical of their attitude . . . is the conversation one time of a stranger that came into the ward. In looking around and seeing that most of them were Latin Americans, he saw these few Anglos there, and one in particular, and he said, 'What is he doing here? He's not Mexican.' One of the members of the ward standing there talking with him said, 'He's more Mexican than we are,' " an answer that pleased Burton.[11]

The branch—and later the ward—was—and continues to be—active. Members held Spanish or Mexican socials, presented operettas, and served Mexican food on holidays. They held dances and dinners for other wards and businesses which raised 80 percent of the money needed to build the meetinghouse in 1951. The Church organization became the main source of cultural activities for members. Without offering any explanation, Mexican American Arturo Rivera Martinez, who was born in Salt Lake City in 1929, explained his and the parents of other teenagers refused to let them attend the largely Catholic Centro Civico Mexicano activities. As a result, "Our social life and most every phase of our life was involved in the Church and in the old Salt Lake Mexican branch."[12]

The socials sometimes blended the cultures. Martinez recalled going to dances where the teenagers did the tango and "folkloric" dances. He remembered piñata parties as well, explaining, "We were able to retain most of our culture." At the same time, he remembered adding European American elements such as Christmas parties with a Santa Claus. He explained, "I guess that wasn't part of the Spanish culture, Mexican culture, but we combined them all." James Vernon Sharp recalled the "intense national pride" of the members. "We celebrated every Mexican holiday." He found this emphasis appropriate, since "part of the reason for the existence of the Mexican branch was so that they could retain some of their past history of their country."[13]

In the 1930s the ward won its stake basketball tournament and placed in an All-Church tournament. In 1959 and 1960 it won the stake road show competition. It also had an excellent Boy Scout program. Members participated in welfare assignments and held dinners to raise money for a building. A group sponsored dinners and invited the community. Frequently over 1,000 attended. The Lucero Ward was the first to fill its quota for the Relief Society building in the 1940s. In the 1950s the ward catered a dinner for several hundred Genealogical Society workers at Lagoon. A ward choir frequently sang at socials. Dances and Christmas parties with piñatas were very popular. The Fiestas de las Piñatas attracted over a thousand people. One year so many came that branch members ran out of food to serve.[14]

Arturo Rivera Martinez remembered people looking down on him and calling him a Mexican. "It got to the point where I was beginning to be ashamed of whom I was. They said it to me in a derogatory form, and this is what I resented." He learned to tell the difference between "good people and those who were ignorant." The prejudice was both overt and subtle; it often came from "those who held high positions in the Church." After World War II he perceived some Mormons as reluctant to trust Mexican leaders. Some Latter-day Saints refused to work with Mexicans, insisting that they were dirty. With these reactions, it is easy to understand why Mexican Saints enjoyed worshipping together where they felt comfortable and understood.[15]

Bishop Burton felt that the ward struggled with national divisions. He explained, "There are countries where the general racial background of the people and their culture is a little more removed from the culture of the basic Spanish-American." A common language, though important, did not automatically guarantee "unity or . . . attraction to each other."[16]

Martinez agreed. The congregation initially had been nearly all Mexican. The change of the ward's name along with status in 1959 reflected a mix of nationalities—ranging from Indians to Europeans. National conflicts carried over into the ward as feelings, suspicion, or stereotypes. Yet natural forces for unity were a common language, the immigrant status for newcomers, minority status, and mutual alienation from Hispanic Catholics.[17]

As a young man, Martinez felt that the Pioneer and Temple View stakes accepted the branch and ward. Stake members considered the branch an asset. Its leaders challenged the other units to meet the Spanish-speaking unit's 80 percent church attendance and 100 percent ward teaching records. Still, "on some other occasions we had the feeling that we were just a burden on them." Martinez had friends from the other wards in the stake, but "most of the time the parents were a little reluctant to let their kids associate with us too closely." As a result, "very rarely would we date anyone from another ward. We did participate in some stake functions with other youth." This policy helped bind the Spanish-speaking youth together. Bishop Burton openly acknowledged a wish to discourage interracial dating as a way of avoiding the problems of interracial marriage.[18]

Although the Church leaders dissolved other Spanish-speaking branches in the Salt Lake Valley in the early 1970s, assigning members to geographical wards, the Lucero Ward continued to operate because there were always new members. Burton said his goals were to hold leadership meetings so that the future leaders would come from "among their own people" and to make the members economically independent. Burton's replacement in 1966, Orlando Rivera, was a Latino American. By 1973 Eduardo Balderas reported fulfillment of Burton's goals: "It's a full-fledged ward, . . . and so the people have the opportunity to run their own ward with their own people. They have enough members so that they can select teachers from among them, also officers for their organizations." Those who followed up as bishop until 1983 when the ward stopped sending in records were also Latino Americans: Elias R. Torres (1978–82) and Jose Angel Alba (1982–).[19] The ward was still operating in 1997.

Cumorah[20]

Initially the Lucero Ward drew its members from all of the Salt Lake Valley. In 1961 it was so large it was split into three: Lucero, Cumorah, and Helaman. The Cumorah Branch, part of the Midvale Stake, was organized by the regional mission leaders. Mission President Golden Buchanan conducted the first meeting on 18 April 1962. Two apostles, Mark E. Petersen and Spencer W. Kimball, along with an Assistant to the Twelve, Boyd K. Packer, also attended. All three spoke with the aid of a translator. Kimball quoted scriptures about the need to build up the Church among the Lamanites and also quoted former Church President John Taylor who had prophesied about the day when the Lamanites would become part of the main church with wards and stakes. Kimball concluded, "We are doing what we are commanded to and fulfilling prophecy"—referring to the work of the regional mission. He concluded: "Let this little branch that starts like an acorn grow big and strong like a mighty oak."

Mark E. Petersen led a discussion about the branch's boundaries, offering 4500 South and 3900 South as northern options. The majority voted for 3900 South, the larger boundary. A second vote made the decision unanimous. Some branch members wanted to name the branch after Anthony W. Ivins, but Petersen said that the Church discouraged naming units after people. Members agreed on Cumorah after the hill where Joseph Smith found the gold plates.

At first the branch met in a Boy Scout log cabin. Later it moved to the Midvale Second Ward building. Mexican American Samuel Victor Miera, a former Spanish American missionary, was branch president from 1967 to 1971. During that time, there were about 200 members from throughout the United States, Central and South America, and Puerto Rico.[21]

The branch cooperated closely with the Lucero Ward. In May 1961 the branch cosponsored a Mexican dinner with the ward; 280 people attended and the branch cleared $308. Many sacrament meeting speakers came from the ward. Among other activities sponsored in 1963 with the stake president's approval were La Fiesta de Los Charros and Fiesta de Las Piñatas. Between 1962 and 1966, the period when a manuscript history is available, the branch also had a choir, a basketball team, occasionally a Primary, and a folk dancing group. Arturo Rivera Martinez and Miera praised Reid Young, a member of the Midvale Stake high council, because of his assistance to the branch and his willingness to lobby for Cumorah with the stake presidency. Martinez called him the branch's patron saint, and Miera compared Young's support to Jacob Hamblin's and Spencer W. Kimball's support of Native Americans.[22]

Despite sometimes unexplained unpleasant "encounters with [European American] members," Cumorah Branch leaders had good relationships with stake and ward officials in the Midvale Stake. All branch meetings were in Spanish. During stake conferences, the branch members met in a separate room and had simultaneous translation. Branch leaders felt while 60 percent of the branch members could have functioned in English, serving the 40 percent who could not was also important.[23]

The level of activity was impressive. For example, on stake 100 percent Sunday School day on 17 March 1963, Cumorah won the stake award with 128 percent attendance. Because so many nonmember children came, the Primary (when it was operating) had over 100 percent attendance. Cumorah also had 100 percent home teaching, 65–75 percent attendance at sacrament meeting, and 50 percent full tithe payers and temple recommend holders. The branch led the stake in contributions and fast offerings.[24]

There were some problems. Branch leaders required proof of legal entry from members. Samuel Victor Miera explained until he became branch president, he assumed all the members were legal U.S. residents. However, he found that was not the case. As a result, he "made sure that the [immigrants] were obeying the law." If the families were in the United States legally, Miera told them, "We'll welcome you in Cumorah. We'll put you to work." If they had come illegally, "then we would advise them, 'All right. Now look. Now you want to stay in the United States. It's much better for you if you go back there and do it right.' " Most returned and then came to the U.S. legally. Only three or four families returned to Mexico and never returned. Miera concluded, "After that all the people in the Cumorah Branch were legal."[25]

There were also some early conflicts among the nationalities from Latin America. But Miera characterized the feeling as "one big family" with any problems being only "a flash in the pan." He continued, "It was soon made clear that we were all in this together and we were going to hang right there, like brothers should. . . . I don't want to make it sound like Camelot. . . . But that is about as close to Camelot as anybody will ever get."[26]

The branch never became a ward because it was small and Church leaders did not consider it permanent.[27] On 14 May 1974, 289 branch members listened to Arturo Rivera Martinez, then a regional representative, tell them that if they would "accept the dissolvement of the branch they [would] grow and progress." After listening to several other talks, "a majority" of the members voted to eliminate the branch. Only a year later in an oral history interview, Martinez pointed out that the centrally imposed policy of disbanding "all of the minority group and foreign language units. . . . didn't work, so now they're going to reorganize a few."[28] In 1997 the Midvale 9th Ward was a Spanish-speaking unit.

El Paso, Texas

In 1910 when Eduardo Balderas was three, his family left Mexico and moved to El Paso, Texas. His father, Jose Apolinar Balderas, a barber, frequently cut the hair of the Mormon elders. The older Balderas and the missionaries hoped for more than hair cuts. The elders wanted the barber to listen to their message; Balderas wanted Spanish-speaking Mormon customers. However, after Balderas heard Mexican Mission President Rey L. Pratt speak, he and his thirteen-year-old son Eduardo joined the LDS Church.[29]

Mary Pratt Parrish, a daughter of Mission President Rey L. Pratt, recalled her early days in El Paso. The branch met in her parents' home, and she said, "The neighbors didn't like it. They couldn't understand why all these Mexican people would come to our home on Sunday morning." All the ward activities were also held in the Pratt home.[30] After the Pratts moved to Los Angeles, Eduardo remembered attending a Spanish-speaking branch with thirty to thirty-five members that met in members' homes. The meetings were sacrament, priesthood, and Sunday School, and a mid-week preaching service for the missionaries and investigators. There were no programs for the children and teenagers. (He did not comment about women.) Eduardo did not remember discrimination from English-speaking members but added, "The Spanish-speaking people, because of their customs and language, prefer to be by themselves."[31]

During the 1920s most branch leaders in the Mexican Mission were Anglo Americans. However, two years after he was baptized, Jose Apolinar Balderas became the branch president in El Paso. Parrish recalled, "He was a spiritual giant. . . . You couldn't be around him ten minutes without feeling that great spiritual depth."[32] Balderas continued in that position for ten years.

When Jose Apolinar Balderas returned to Mexico, his twenty-five-year-old son, Eduardo, replaced him. The branch then had 75 to 100 members. Because the branch was so small, it had limited auxiliary programs.[33] When Eduardo left in 1939 to be a translator in Salt Lake City, the branch had a chapel that would hold 150 members.[34] By 1951 it had 233 members and a full auxiliary program.[35]

In 1952 Apostles Harold B. Lee and Spencer W. Kimball organized it as the El Paso Third Ward, reportedly the first Spanish ward in the Church. Gullermo Balderas, Eduardo's nephew, then branch president, became the first bishop.[36] Very few records exist for the El Paso Third Ward. The manuscript history includes information starting in 1976 and ending in 1983, but there are only reports of releases and sustainings. Spanish American Mission records up to 1967 give very brief reports of branch activities.

Duane W. Francis, a Anglo American missionary from Bountiful, discussed numerous problems in the Third Ward in the 1970s. For him the ward was too large (over one thousand members) and the members were "cliquish." As a result, he preferred to take his investigators to English-speaking wards. But English-speaking ward mission leaders did not want to provide classes for the Spanish-speaking members.[37]

Francis's views are biased because his entire focus was working with nonmembers and trying to convert them and have them remain active in the El Paso wards. His youth and enthusiasm limited his perception of the wards. It is possible though to compare some of his ideas with those of the Spanish-speaking members. For example, Francis complained that the Mexican American members were "real big on the 'brown is beautiful' theme."[38] Members of the Associacion Cultural Mexico Americana, an organization created in El Paso in 1969, explained their views. According to the officers, the association was established to express cultural concerns and share them with church leaders. It also wanted to encourage the use of Spanish language at stake activities and show European Americans the problems of stereotypes. Other goals included providing activities that strengthened Mexican American culture.

In a 1970 letter to Church President Joseph Fielding Smith, the association explained, "We sincerely pray that this letter is not perceived as the wild rantings of a militant minority group, but rather as a plea for understanding and consideration of our desperate situation." The letter then explained problems with general Church programs such as genealogy, MIA, and Relief Society which were all presented from an "Anglo-Saxon" point of view. To help deal with these problems, the members asked for social activities that included their cultural background in their own facility. They complained about attending English-speaking wards where they were not given callings or asked to participate. They stressed, "We feel that because of the beliefs we hold and have held for a long time that we are being ostracized. We are classified as problems that can be ignored, and if we can't be ignored we can be castigated by being labeled rebels, traitors, apostates, intellectual snobs, and openly denounced as being possessed of the devil." Instead, the group felt that they were trying to be members and maintain their culture. "We do not feel that [the] added burden of acculturation should be a condition for developing in the gospel."[39]

The struggle between Anglo American members and missionaries like Francis and Latino American Mormons like those in the association continued just as they carried on in the larger Mexican American and European American communities of El Paso. According to Eduardo Balderas, members of "this minority movement—the Chicanos" felt they were "not given the same opportunities for occupying positions of responsibility in the American missions and stakes." He added that his nephew had trouble with these members but added, "When anyone stands up against them, especially one of their own people, they are immediately dubbed as 'gringo' lovers."[40] Balderas spent many years at Mormon Church headquarters as a translator and probably spoke from that position. Like many other Mexican Americans, he had adjusted to the Mormon views. Unfortunately, he did not explain what being a "gringo lover" meant to those giving that name and those being tagged that way.

There are no records to determine what has happened since the 1970s. Francis did talk about stake suggestions in the 1970s to transfer the Spanish-speaking work to Ciudad Juarez across the border in Mexico. Other reports in 1997 suggest that option is still considered sometimes.[41] In 1997, though, there were five Spanish-speaking wards in the El Paso area, almost enough for a stake.

Tucson, Arizona

Anglo American Leslie O. Brewer, who had served a Spanish-speaking mission in Los Angeles during the 1920s, worked in Tucson as a teacher during the 1940s. He recalled that usually there were only two English-speaking branches in town, with an occasional third Spanish-speaking branch which opened and closed, depending on the success of the missionary work and the activity of the Spanish-speaking members.

When it was operating, Brewer explained, "If you were a Mexican and didn't attend the Mexican branch, you were a heretic. You were an absolute traitor." This social pressure, he felt, sometimes disadvantaged Hispanic members and cites the case of a Sister Ortega who, "to this day, blames that for the fact that she lost her whole family. They all spoke English and if she had been allowed to let them go to these English-speaking branches she might have kept them in the Church." Instead, only Sister Ortega and one daughter were active in 1973.[42]

Tucson Stake leaders disbanded the Spanish branch in 1950. Spanish-speaking members were still meeting with wards in 1958 when the West Spanish American Mission was formed, and most felt that arrangement was best. Natalie Ortega explained, "I feel that there are more opportunities available to Spanish members in the English-speaking wards. The white people help us progress." Henry Acereto pointed out, "I cannot speak English very well yet." But he still felt welcomed by the Tucson European American Mormons and continued, "I much prefer to meet with the white brothers in the English wards." Some members like Lupe Robles, a mother of ten children, said she understood the English sermons but she would like a separate Sunday School class in Spanish. No one who spoke at the meeting, however, favored separate Spanish-speaking branches.[43]

Despite these reports, a year late a study found only seven of twenty-eight families active or partially active.[44] When Brewer became a stake president in Tucson, Apostle Spencer W. Kimball asked him to form an independent Spanish American branch because "we weren't taking care of the social needs of our Spanish-speaking members. Even though they spoke enough English to get along in an Anglo ward they still weren't socially well adjusted and were dropping out." Members could choose whether they wanted to attend the ward or the branch, but most went to the branch. Those who went to the geographical wards occasionally helped with the Spanish branch. Brewer concluded that the process worked, adding when he was interviewed in 1973 that the branch was "a fairly strong organization."[45]

The Tucson Spanish-speaking congregation was later dissolved. When Mexican American Ignacio Garcia, a Ph.D. student at the University of Arizona, moved to Tucson in 1982, a new Spanish-speaking ward had only been in operation for about a year. The bishop, Mexican American Richard R. Gomez, was a vice president of the Hughes Corporation. Garcia explained that Gomez, who had been attending geographical wards, had been asked to preside over the ward because there were very few priesthood leaders available. The men and women who had presided over the branch and the auxiliaries in the 1930s were no longer active.

Gomez served as bishop of the Tucson Spanish-speaking ward for nine years. During that time, Ignacio Garcia explained, while the ward functioned well, there was always a struggle to integrate on the stake level. Ward members did not participate in stake activities and felt very little identity with the stake.

In 1990 Ignacio Garcia was called as the bishop of the ward. Almost immediately he told the stake leaders that the Spanish-speaking ward was not a "minor league" where members attended until they spoke English enough to move to the "major league" geographical wards. Garcia also explained that the ward would participate in stake programs, but the Spanish-speaking members would not be the source of entertainment for English-speaking members. As a result of working with the stake and planning joint activities where Spanish-speaking and English-speaking members shared food and talent, Garcia felt that the relationship with the stake improved.

Before Garcia became bishop, youth classes had been in English. Garcia moved all lessons to Spanish. He felt having the youth lessons in English created a division between the young people and their parents. He and the other ward leaders also worried about the splits in families they saw in Mesa where the Spanish-speaking and English-speaking wards had separate sacrament meetings but all the Latino youth went to the English-speaking wards for auxiliaries. Garcia focused on the youth programs, and within two and a half years bragged that he had the most successful scouting program in the region and a Young Men/Young Women program that European American parents wanted their children to attend.

Garcia also felt it was important that all the meetings be in Spanish because it gave a chance for all members to participate. Some had recently come from Mexico where they had been leaders in their wards, but they could not take part in church meetings in English. Garcia did not worry whether the members were in the United States illegally. He explained, "My ward council was forty percent undocumented. They were good people. They were the most dedicated. I called them to leadership positions. Some of them couldn't understand the language. But they were very efficient in the things they did."

When Garcia finished his Ph.D. program at the University of Arizona, he moved to Texas to teach. The bishops that followed were also well educated and continued to focus on the Spanish-speaking branch. However, in April 1997 Garcia's sister-in-law informed him that all members of the Spanish-speaking ward who could speak English had been asked to go to the geographical ward. The ward was only for those who could not communicate in English.[46]

Sacramento, California

Juan Ramon Martinez and his wife Rumalda Gonzales Martinez, LDS members originally from New Mexico who had also lived in Monticello, Utah, moved to Sacramento in the early 1950s. They were concerned when their fourteen children stopped attending the English-speaking branches, so they asked Church leaders if they could be part of the Spanish American Mission. Leaders agreed and created a Spanish-speaking branch. In June 1951, fifty-eight members of the Martinez family were attending the branch.

When a mission reorganization took California out of the Spanish American Mission in 1951, Sacramento Branch members received a promise from Spencer W. Kimball, then an apostle touring the mission, that the branch would not change.[47] But it did. At a branch conference on 9 September 1951, just after the stake took over, the English-speaking leaders asked the members to hold their meetings in English. In 1957 these leaders decided that they would conduct the auxiliary meetings or have branch members go to those meetings in a ward.[48]

When the West Spanish American Mission was created in 1958, the branch again experienced changes. At an open meeting many branch members "felt that it would be better to go back to the Spanish language in the branch meeting." Kimball urged the branch members to teach their children Spanish as part of their "heritage" and added, "The Church will never require you to learn [English] to know the Gospel; the lessons will be furnished in Spanish." He asked the stake presidency to develop leadership among the Spanish-speaking people and to hold branch Sunday School and sacrament meetings in Spanish, insisting that the majority should not make a decision that ignored the minority. The branch should also have its own auxiliary meetings with help from stake missionaries. But, Kimball added, the Mutual-aged teenagers could go to the English-speaking wards. Members could hold home Primary if transportation were a problem. As a result, the Sacramento Branch continued to hold meetings in Spanish and sponsor activities including tamale sales and Mexican-style dinners, sometimes for the entire stake.[49]

When the Church conducted a survey in 1959, they found 11,000 Spanish-speaking people in Sacramento and 9,000 in the surrounding county, a large potential convert pool. About 25 percent of the Broderick neighborhood residents were Spanish-speaking, but the rest lived throughout the city. The branch was part of the North Sacramento Stake, and members had to travel twenty to thirty minutes to get to an inadequate chapel. One member said that the stake leaders never visited the branch.[50]

Since the Spanish-speaking people were not centralized, the mission president moved the elders using that language away from the city. Missionaries assigned to San Jose and later Stockton visited once a week. The local stakes started providing stake missionaries who spoke Spanish.[51] There are no additional minutes for Spanish-speaking congregations in Sacramento. There was a Spanish-speaking ward in the city in 1997.

Los Angeles, California

In Los Angeles, California, the Mormon Hispanic American population grew very rapidly. When Church leaders transferred the Spanish-speaking missionary work and branches from the Spanish American Mission in 1951, the California Mission did not leave the proselyting to the stake missionaries. Instead, the president assigned six full-time missionaries to work in Spanish in 1953. In April they started conducting a Spanish Sunday School class as part of the Adams Ward. The efforts were not successful at first. Few people attended, and those who did were more interested in hearing Spanish than in learning about the gospel.

Eventually more Hispanics joined the Church, and the local leaders formed Spanish-speaking branches in Glendale and Belvedere. Missionary efforts among the Spanish-speaking people increased in 1958 when Church leaders formed the West Spanish American Mission, but the branches remained in the stakes.[52]

In 1959 the memberships of Spanish-speaking Saints were moved to the Belvedere Ward. Apostle Kimball who was in charge of the first meeting remembered, "So far as could be noted, the voting of the Spanish-speaking people was unanimous. Some had briefly expressed sentimental reasons why it was hard to leave their old surroundings in which they had grown up but the old chapel and recreation and classroom facilities of the Belvedere Ward will be much better for them." Silvino Seanez who had been the Spanish branch president became bishop of the Belvedere Ward with Maximino Diaz and Regnaldo I. Garcia as counselors. Kimball added that the voting in the English-speaking ward was not unanimous, although he did not explain why.[53]

During the 1960s, revolutions in Central and South America brought more Spanish-speaking refugees to the United States, and many settled in western Los Angeles. Some were already Latter-day Saints; others joined in the United States. They did not have a place nearby to attend church in their native language and many did not have transportation to the Glendale branch. In 1964 Orestes Rodriguez, a Wilshire Ward member who spoke Spanish and English, asked Bishop Varnell Rozsa to have a Spanish Sunday School class. By the end of the year, the Spanish-speaking members had a group and held their own sacrament meeting.

In 1965 newly sustained stake president Anglo American Winfield Q. Cannon focused on the Spanish people. He felt they, along with the Koreans who were moving into the area, should learn the gospel in their own language and have places where they could worship together. In June 1966 he organized the Spanish-speaking group into a dependent branch. Four months later in October it became an independent branch, "acting on a recommendation of the First Presidency."[54]

When Church leaders discontinued the West Spanish American Mission in 1970, the California Mission again had elders and sisters who taught in Spanish. Through their efforts and the steady immigration to the area, the branch grew slowly, eventually outgrowing its meeting space in the Wilshire Ward baptismal room. At first the branch met in the annex of the Los Angeles Stake Center. It continued to grow and soon met in the Wilshire Ward chapel.[55]

By April 1978 nearly 500 people regularly attended sacrament meeting in the Los Angeles Spanish Branch, an increase of over 300 percent in five years. Church leaders divided the branch, creating Los Angeles Third Ward and Los Angeles Fourth Branch. By September, Fourth Branch became a ward.[56]

The Los Angeles Stake continued its efforts to work with the Spanish-speaking members, especially after President Spencer W. Kimball spoke at an area conference in 1980 and asked the members to help the Hispanics. Leaders called Spanish-speaking members to stake assignments and provided training classes. By June 1983 there were almost a thousand Hispanic members in the stake, most in the Los Angeles Third Ward. Church leaders created a third Spanish-speaking ward, the Los Angeles Sixth Ward.[57]

The Church also grew rapidly among Hispanics throughout the greater Los Angeles area. As a result, leaders organized wards and branches in Santa Monica (1969), Huntington Beach (1978), and Inglewood (1980). By 1983 there were seventeen units between Torrance and Hacienda Heights. At a special training session, four stake presidents made plans to organize the first Spanish-speaking stake in the United States. Some leaders and Spanish members suggested the idea in 1972, but many feared there were not enough Spanish-speaking priesthood leaders. By 1983 sufficient Hispanics had served in stake positions to understand church procedure.[58]

General church leaders approved the organization of the stake in 1984. In June Howard W. Hunter of the Council of Twelve, Robert L. Backman of the First Quorum of Seventy and Executive Administrator of the Southern California Area, and John K. Carmack, a member of the First Quorum of Seventy and former leader in the Los Angeles Stake, participated in the first meeting. At first the new Huntington Park West Stake had seven wards with over 2,200 members. Rafael N. Seminario, a former bishop of the Los Angeles Third Ward, became the first stake president. Seminario commented during the meeting, "We're happy the Brethren have seen fit to form the stake, giving us the opportunity to be in leadership positions. We are going to have many challenges, but we think we have a lot of brothers and sisters who are ready and willing to put forth the extra effort that it requires to bring forth the work. . . . We have had the opportunity to work in the Anglo wards. We have learned a lot and this is probably the best test for everyone to see how much we have learned."[59]

Spanish-speaking membership continued to grow. By 1995 five stakes where Spanish was the primary language dotted the Southern California area. These stakes provided all the regular programs of the Church including single wards. Ward members were extremely active; often with sacrament meeting above 100 percent. Because of the steadily increasing membership, wards were large and divided frequently. In April 1997 there were rumors, though, that one of the Spanish-speaking stakes was being dissolved.[60]

Provo/Orem, Utah

Other areas throughout the United States with significant Hispanic populations stopped short of creating stakes. As in Southern California, the wards were large and had very high attendance. To keep the units manageable, Church leaders frequently divided them. In an area like Provo/Orem, Utah, many Spanish-speaking immigrants were already Latter-day Saints who chose to come to the state to be close to the Church headquarters. As members and missionaries shared the gospel message with their neighbors, the number of local converts grew steadily.

A Mexican branch was organized in Provo in 1960. Enoc Q. Flores, a Mexican American from the Mormon colonies in Mexico, came to Provo in 1964 after serving a mission. He remembered then there was a small Spanish branch in Provo with fewer than fifty members. He worked as the ward clerk and a counselor in the branch presidency. "I went through all the organizations. I was a teacher. I was the elder's quorum president. I was the Sunday School president. Almost everything that you can imagine I had the opportunity of doing there because there were not a lot of us."[61]

Flores eventually left the branch to attend a geographical ward. In 1981 when the branch became a ward, he was asked to return as the first bishop. He recalled, "It was a great experience to see the development and the growth that the people had done. They were mostly new people because the ward was used as a spring board or as an entry into the Church. Once the people learned the language they would move into the different wards."[62]

In 1991 a Spanish-speaking ward met in a chapel at 800 North and 500 West in Provo. The ward was so large that at a missionary farewell the congregation overflowed from the chapel to the back of the cultural hall. Ricardo Diaz, a Mexican American BYU student, was attending the ward then. He explained, "The 33rd ward is the best ward that I've ever been to . . . because it is fully active." The ward sponsored two or three activities a week. There were so many members that they were "just asking for jobs." In addition to all the members, there were often visitors who came consistently but left their memberships in geographical wards.[63]

Diaz was interviewed in March 1991. He explained that the ward was so large "we should be splitting this Sunday. That should be really fun. I bet as soon as that starts we are going to have two large wards because there are many people who have stopped coming because it was so big."[64] The split did come that month, and the new Serrano Ward became part of the Provo South Stake. In 1996 the Serrano Ward was split again, and in a Churchwide effort to standardize names became the East Bay Second Ward.

The East Bay Second Ward and a branch for deaf members throughout Utah County continued as part of the Provo Utah South Stake. To meet the needs of the deaf members at stake conferences, a translator stood on the rostrum and signed. Spanish-speaking members listened through portable headsets. High councilors included both deaf and Spanish-speaking men. The stake presidency provided translators and signers for high council meetings. Hispanic member Arlene Fuentes appreciated those efforts, adding that in her stake there were no Spanish-speaking high councilors.[65]

Even with these special efforts to include Spanish-speaking members, the Provo South Stake still had problems. Ward Primary leaders had to bring their own translators to stake auxiliary meetings and, as a result, rarely came. Latino Americans also had a hard time listening to the two-hour stake conferences through headsets. The singing was only in English. English and Spanish-speaking members could not talk because of the language barrier. There were essentially two meetings going on in the same room with little interaction—mainly smiles—between the two groups.[66] In 1997 there were at least six Spanish-speaking wards in the Provo/Orem area.

Buhl, Idaho

An interesting example of a Spanish-speaking branch in an area with few members was organized in Buhl, Idaho, in 1983. It technically had no boundaries and was the only branch for Latino Americans within 3,500 square miles. The branch served agricultural workers who came from Mexico and Latin America to work for the local farmers. In 1992 about sixty-five people attended every week; there were fifteen active families. Over time the branch presidents had been European Americans and

Hispanics. All meetings were in Spanish. The Primary went to an English-speaking ward.

When the branch was organized, Randall Morgan, a European American freelance film producer who spoke Spanish, was assigned as the high council representative to the branch. Since the Morgan family members wanted to attend services together, they decided to go to the branch and learn Spanish. (The Morgans had six children at that time, ranging in age from newborn to twelve. They later had another child.) Ellen Morgan, who attended the Spanish-speaking branch from age eight to nineteen, affirmed, "I believe that if every LDS white American had the opportunity to attend an ethnic congregation for a few years, the Church within the United States would be different. It would be more missionary minded, more tolerant, less tradition bound, and more dynamic."

The Morgan family loved their opportunities to work in the branch. By age nineteen, Ellen had been branch librarian, a counselor in the Young Women's program, a Relief Society teacher, and, very frequently, an organist and chorister. She accepted and appreciated the culture of a group of people frequently misunderstood in rural Idaho. Although she attended a BYU English-speaking ward in 1996, she missed the Spanish experience. She explained, "It required some adjustment to get used to a BYU ward, to sit in the back row and not really be needed." She continued, "Although there are definite advantages to being in a strong ward, I still miss singing the hymns in Spanish and always notice that the sacrament prayers sound different." She then changed the traditional Mormon phrase that "the Church is the same wherever you go" to "the Gospel is the same wherever you go but the Church is different. I am glad I've been able to experience those differences."[67]

Randall Morgan was the branch president when his daughter Anna went on a mission in 1992 and still held that position in 1997. In 1997 his wife DeAnna talked about the strengths and weaknesses of the branch. Like her daughter Ellen, DeAnna said she and her family "love the people, the branch, the language, the cultural differences, the opportunity to serve and to learn." The branch benefitted the Latinos because it is "an opportunity to worship in their own language, to have important leadership and teaching callings, to function within a little micro-cosmic model of the Church."

While DeAnna Morgan praised the branch, she also recognized its weaknesses. Most of the members are new converts. Many live in poverty; most are uneducated. The members work with the missionaries and there is a high conversion rate. According to Ellen, the branch has the most converts in the stake. But both DeAnna and Ellen point out that these members do not stay long. "The greatest problem our branch has always faced is that the seed falls, the plant speedily springs up, but it is soon plucked up. The inactivity rate is fast and high."

DeAnna Morgan enjoyed the branch fiestas. "We eat great tamales and break piñatas." She did not see conflicts between the Spanish-speaking members from many countries, although, she said, "Sometimes a little national pride is seen." The Hispanic and European Americans assigned to work with the branch had "comfortable relationships." Despite the high inactivity rate, there were always "highlights" in the branch: "A strong new member, a once weak member taking a leadership position, a family going to the temple, etc. The usual wonderful victories, but somehow more exciting in the branch where so many members are struggling."[68]

Summary

Church leaders started Spanish-speaking branches throughout the Southwest, first as part of the Mexican Mission and then as part of other missions or local stakes. The LDS Church Archives list of local records includes nearly one hundred Spanish-speaking wards and branches across the United States from Anaheim, California, to Morristown, New Jersey. These branch records vary from incomplete to almost non-existent, so it is difficult to trace their history. But the information in this chapter, collected from manuscript histories and oral histories, depicts some successes and problems that ethnic-language branches typically experienced.

Despite the differences (services that were all or partly in ethnic languages, Mexican food at parties, etc.), these wards conformed closely to American models in structure, procedures, staffing, and curriculum, enabling observers to characterize them by the approving phrase, "The Church is the same all over the world." Their very existence, however, frequently sparked debates about whether separate branches should exist.

Notes

1. Spencer W. Kimball Journal, 22 and 25 March 1963, in private possession. Used by permission of the family.

2. German-speaking Ward, University West Stake, Tape of organizational meeting, 30 January 1963, LDS Church Archives, Historical Department, Church of Jesus Christ of Latter-day Saints, Salt Lake City, Utah. (Hereinafter referred to as LDS Church Archives.)

3. Oakland Stake, Manuscript History, 1988, LDS Church Archives.

4. Giles H. Florence, Jr., "City of Angels," *Ensign* 22 (September 1992): 36.

5. "Three Rivera Sisters Devoted Workers in the Mexican Branch," *Church News*, 30 June 1956, 16.

6. James Vernon Sharp, Oral History, interviewed by Gordon Irving, 1972, 37, LDS Church Archives.

7. Arturo Martinez, Oral History, interviewed by Gordon Irving, 1975, 24, LDS Church Archives; Lucero Ward, Manuscript History, LDS Church Archives.

8. Sharp, Oral History, 25, 35–36.

9. Lucero Ward, Manuscript History; "Pres. Clark Dedicates Mexican Branch Chapel," *Church News*, 20 June 1951, 2.

10. Lucero Ward, Manuscript History.

11. Robert Henry Burton, Oral History, interviewed by William G. Hartley, 1972, 3–4, LDS Church Archives.

12. Martinez, Oral History, 17–19.

13. Ibid., 17–19, 25; Sharp, Oral History, 38.

14. Burton, Oral History, 4–7; Martinez, Oral History, 29, 79; Lucero Ward, Manuscript History.

15. Martinez, Oral History, 13–15.

16. Burton, Oral History, 21–22.

17. Martinez, Oral History, 22–23.

18. Ibid., 30; Burton, Oral History, 15.

19. Martinez, Oral History, 78; Burton, Oral History, 6; Eduardo Balderas, Oral History, interviewed by Gordon Irving, 1973, 76, LDS Church Archives; Lucero Ward, Manuscript History.

20. Unless otherwise cited, the information on the Cumorah Branch comes from the Cumorah Branch, Manuscript History, LDS Church Archives. The Archives also has a tape of the organizational meeting. Transcripts of the meeting in English and Spanish appear in the Manuscript History.

21. Samuel Victor Miera, Oral History, interviewed by Gordon Irving, 1975–76, 51, 54, LDS Church Archives.

22. Ibid., 56–57; Martinez, Oral History, 81–82.

23. Miera, Oral History, 55, 58, 61–62

24. Ibid., 55.

25. Ibid., 59–61.

26. Ibid., 72.

27. Ibid., 58.

28. Martinez, Oral History, 262.

29. Balderas, Oral History, 6.

30. Mary Pratt Parrish, Oral History, interviewed by Gordon Irving, 1973, 17, LDS Church Archives.

31. Balderas, Oral History, 3.

32. Parrish, Oral History, 21.

33. Balderas, Oral History, 6–33.

34. Ibid., 13.

35. Ivie Jones, Papers, LDS Church Archives.

36. Spanish American Mission, 21 September 1952, 13 December 1953, LDS Church Archives.

37. Duane W. Francis, Oral History, interviewed by Gordon Irving, 1977, 37–45, LDS Church Archives.

38. Ibid., 40.

39. Associacion Cultural Mexico Americana Letter and File, LDS Church Archives.

40. Balderas, Oral History, 78.

41. Francis, Oral History, 44–45; comments from Ignacio Garcia to author.

42. Leslie O. and Nina Brewer, Oral History, interviewed by Ronald K. Esplin, 1973, 12, LDS Church Archives.

43. West Spanish American Mission, Manuscript History, 12 March 1958, LDS Church Archives.

44. [Roland G. and Elizabeth E. Kaiser], "Population Survey Pertaining to Spanish-Speaking People in California and Arizona, 1958–1961," Special Collections, 6, Harold B. Lee Library, Brigham Young University, Provo, Utah.

45. Brewer, Oral History, 18.

46. Ignacio Garcia, Conversation with Jessie Embry, 4 April 1997, transcript in the Charles Redd Center for Western Studies, Brigham Young University.

47. Ivie Jones, Papers.

48. Spanish Branch, Sacramento Stake, Manuscript History, 1951–65, LDS Church Archives.

49. Ibid.; West Spanish American Mission, Manuscript History.

50. "Population Survey," 14.

51. Ibid., Appendix, 1.

52. Chad Orton, *More Faith than Fear: The Los Angeles Stake Story* (Salt Lake City: Bookcraft, 1987), 284–285.

53. Kimball Journal, 26 April 1959.

54. Orton, 240, 285–87; Los Angeles Spanish Branch, 1966, LDS Church Archives.

55. Orton, 289–90.

56. Ibid., 295.

57. Ibid., 197, 298–99, 302.

58. Ibid., 303.

59. Ibid., 304–305.

60. Garcia, Conversation. Other conversations suggest this process is being rethought.

61. Enoc Q. Flores, Oral History, interviewed by Esmeralda Meraz, 1991, 6–7, LDS Hispanic American Oral History Project, Charles Redd Center for Western Studies, Manuscript Division, Harold B. Lee Library, Provo, Utah (hereinafter cited as LDS Hispanic American).

62. Ibid.

63. Ricardo Diaz, Oral History, interviewed by Esmeralda Meraz, 1991, 24, LDS Hispanic American.

64. Ibid.

65. Arlene Fuentes, Oral History, interviewed by Andrea Van Wagenen, 1992, 20, LDS Hispanic American; Author's observations.

66. Author's observations.

67. Reports by Anna Morgan and Ellen Morgan, in possession of author.

68. Letter from DeAnna Morgan to author, 19 February 1997.

CHAPTER FOUR

SHIFTING CHURCH POLICY

Mission Policies

Maintaining non-English language missions and branches was always a struggle because some General Authorities preferred integration. But Apostle Spencer W. Kimball strongly supported keeping them open. In 1964 after visiting Grant M. Burbidge, president of the West Spanish American Mission, Kimball wrote, "I was glad to know that he felt very strongly that we should keep our Spanish-speaking branches intact, feeling that certainly they would go to pieces if they were required to go to the Anglo wards and branches. And as for the mission, he felt positively that it would practically terminate the conversions, at least they would be greatly reduced, and that is nearly unthinkable that we would give up the mission or integrate by requirement the Anglo and Spanish-speaking branches."[1]

However, some members of Spencer W. Kimball's Indian and Minority Group Committee, composed of other apostles and some church members, felt that separate branches encouraged segregation. They argued people from different cultures needed to meet and know each other as individuals.[2] Following established procedure, Kimball rarely mentioned what happened in Council of Twelve meetings in his journal. However, he broke the tradition on 3 February 1966 because he was concerned about attempts to eliminate the ethnic branches and the language missions. He wrote: "Among others was the matter of the possible integration of the minority group branches with the Anglo branches and the possible combination . . . of the missions, doing away with the Spanish-speaking missions in the United States. . . . I vigorously protested and while several of the brethren seemed to feel the other way would be better, I was so vigorous in my protestation that the President did not take a vote on it but asked us to return with the matter next week." He continued, "While it would be easier, more adaptable to administration, I feel sure we would lose ground and many of our members and cease to grow as fast as we have done."[3]

Despite Kimball's concerns, the administrative changes eventually came. In 1967 the Church leaders reorganized the Spanish American Mission. Dean L. Larsen, then president, led the Texas South Mission. The focus of the new mission was still to work with the Spanish-speaking people in South Texas. Other parts of the former Spanish American Mission became part of the Texas and Western States missions.[4]

This arrangement did not last long. In 1970 the Church ended all separate Spanish-speaking missions, likely in an effort to provide administrative clarity about jurisdiction. California elders and sisters assigned to English-speaking missions were teaching Hispanic investigators with few English skills rather than referring them to their Spanish-speaking counterparts. John K. Edmunds, who became president of the California Mission in 1969, talked about the competition between the missionaries. There were many mixed marriages where one partner was Anglo American and the other was Latino American. The two missions agreed that the nationality of the father would determine who should teach the investigators. This plan worked in theory, but Spanish speaking elders did not usually turn over "golden investigators" to the English-speaking elders nor the reverse. "There was a little jealousy and rivalry between them, but it was just human nature."[5]

Former presidents of the Spanish American and West Spanish American missions disagreed about the decision to eliminate the missions. Burbidge simply said that it was right if the Brethren did it but added that he hoped the Spanish speaking people could take part in the Church activities and not become only "listening people."[6] Leland Perry, the first president of the West Spanish American Mission, agreed but saw more potential problems. He recommended that a mission counselor work with just the Spanish-speaking missionaries. He continued, "I'm sure the Brethren know what they're doing. I don't mean to criticize that. I just see some problems there and I think we'll always have them."[7] Harold Bowman, a past president of the Spanish American Mission, however, said, "I thoroughly feel that it's a mistake. I don't mean to criticize, but I feel that and I've had some of the members tell me since. They go to these meetings and they invite them, . . . but they sit back. They don't take the interest that they would before."[8]

Other ethnic missions were also eliminated. Since the ethnic congregations in Salt Lake City were active members of stakes and stake missionaries could talk to nonmembers, the Salt Lake Regional Mission was closed in 1967. In 1972 the First Presidency—Harold B. Lee, President—also dissolved the Southwest Indian Mission and created new missions with geographical boundaries. The First Presidency stressed, though, "Proselyting languages other than English are not to be neglected."[9]

The elimination of ethnic missions did not, of course, eliminate proselyting efforts with these groups in the United States. Geographical missions had developed ways of working with non-English speaking minorities in the 1960s, and these efforts sometimes increased when the Church leaders closed the language missions in 1970 and 1972. As one example, John K. Edmunds, president of the California Mission, appointed David G. Clark, a former mission president of the Guatemala-El Salvador Mission, as his counselor. Clark worked with the Spanish-speaking missionaries and laid the foundation for joint missionary work among the English-speaking Americans and Hispanic people in the area.[10]

Daniel Robins, who served in the California North Mission from 1971 to 1973, started out teaching English-speaking and Spanish-speaking people, but later worked only with Latinos. He estimated that Sacramento had between 75,000 and 80,000 people with Spanish surnames, Smaller towns had Latino populations between 75 and 2,000 in his mission. Most were Mexicans, but there were also people from Chile, Central American countries, and Peru. Robins saw both advantages and disadvantages in each of the two mission systems. While he was not sure it was good to have a mission within a mission, he felt having a separate organization would have made it easier for him to contact Latin people. He was "always jealous" of those missionaries who had served in a Spanish-speaking mission.[11]

In 1972 Michael Landon served in a Spanish-speaking area of Los Angeles while waiting for his Brazilian visa. Though all the missionaries were part of the same mission, he found a division between the "Anglo" and the "Sp Am" missionaries. The Spanish-speaking elders sometimes took a superior attitude because they had learned a language. As with the separate missions, the elders spent all of their time contacting people with Hispanic surnames. On rainy days they went to the library and checked directories arranged by address to find where Hispanics lived since it was sometimes an advantage to go to a door already knowing the person's name. The elders talked only to Latinos. One elder handed out cards with the address of the nearest church when he knocked on the door of non-Spanish speaking people.[12]

Before 1969 missionaries learned the language "on the job." The language training missions created that year for all elders and sisters who taught in a language other than their native tongue improved teaching efforts with non-English speaking groups. By 1983 more than six hundred full-time missionaries were working with minorities in the United States.[13]

Changing Policies on Ethnic Branches

In October 1972 the First Presidency under the direction of President Harold B. Lee issued a circular letter asking all stake, ward, and branch leaders to be conscious of "racial, language, or cultural groups," authorizing stakes and wards to organize special classes where language barriers existed. If there were a greater need, a stake could ask the Quorum of Twelve to organize a branch. Stakes reacted differently to this 1972 letter. Some, like Oakland, dissolved their special units, including a Spanish branch. Others, like the Los Angeles Stake, requested permission to form a language branch, but the General Authorities denied their request. Church leaders also dissolved several branches in the Salt Lake Valley including the Cumorah Branch in 1974. Church translator Eduardo Balderas added that the General Authorities wanted the members to "become incorporated and affiliated with their wards" after they learned English.[14]

Golden Buchanan reacted negatively to these changes, believing that the General Authorities were eliminating all non-English programs in the United States. In an oral history interview in 1975, he referred to a "new handbook [that] says that we should integrate." With this shift in policy, he felt, "There should be a fellowshipping program set up, and if there's a group of people that are not feeling comfortable, they should have special attention, maybe special classes and so on."[15]

A rare exception, although not the only one, was in Provo. Enoc Q. Flores, who had grown up in the Mormon colonies in Mexico, remembered that the 1972 order to end language branches came as "a complete opposite of what they had done ten years before." He was a member of the branch presidency of a Spanish-speaking unit in Provo when the 1972 circular letter arrived. He and the other members of the branch presidency wrote to the General Authorities, describing the reasons for the branch. Flores explained in an oral history that he felt the letter convinced Church leaders to leave the branch open.[16]

Apparently Sunday School classes in ethnic language were not enough. Buchanan asserted—and others probably shared his views—that the Church did not do a good job of taking care of minorities and immigrants during that time. Anglo American Stewart Durrant, who worked with the

Church's Lamanite and Minority Members Committee, said that many members stopped attending when there were no ethnic branches.[17]

This policy was reversed in 1977 when the Church announced a Basic Unit Plan. The new program outlined a simplified branch organization which included only essential positions and programs. It was designed so that a very small group of members could have a congregation that met their basic spiritual needs. Though the program was initially set up for Native Americans, especially those on reservations, committee member Stewart Durrant saw it as a blessing to all people who did not have enough people to have a fully developed church program. Spencer W. Kimball, by then Church President, acknowledged in the Regional Representatives seminar in 1980, "Many challenges face all of us as we fellowship and teach the gospel to the cultural and minority groups living in our midst. . . . When special attention of some kind is not provided for these people, we lose them."[18]

Three years later Kimball declared the programs a success. He wrote to regional representatives and stake and mission presidents, "Where this program has been used we have met with very encouraging success particularly among the minority groups. Where before many were not enjoying full activity in the Church, we now have many smaller branches led by local leaders with increased participation."[19]

Although many people no doubt felt that the policy was meeting a long-standing need, Enoc Flores, whose Spanish branch in Provo had survived the general shut down, now felt that the revival of ethnic branches "went a little overboard. They wanted everybody that was from a different culture to have the gospel taught in their own language. Then we saw a whole bunch of Vietnamese, Hmong, Korean, Japanese, and all of the Asian branches that filled the valley up in Salt Lake and even here in Provo in our stake and in other stakes." He did not explain why he felt this was going "overboard."[20]

Future Policies

In 1992 there were at least 405 foreign-language wards and branches in the United States and over half were Spanish-speaking. (See map.) That number had grown to at least 533 by 1997, and at least two-thirds were Spanish-speaking. In several places there were also foreign-language stakes including, among others, the Spanish-speaking stakes in the Los Angeles

Mormon Spanish Speaking Congregations, 1996

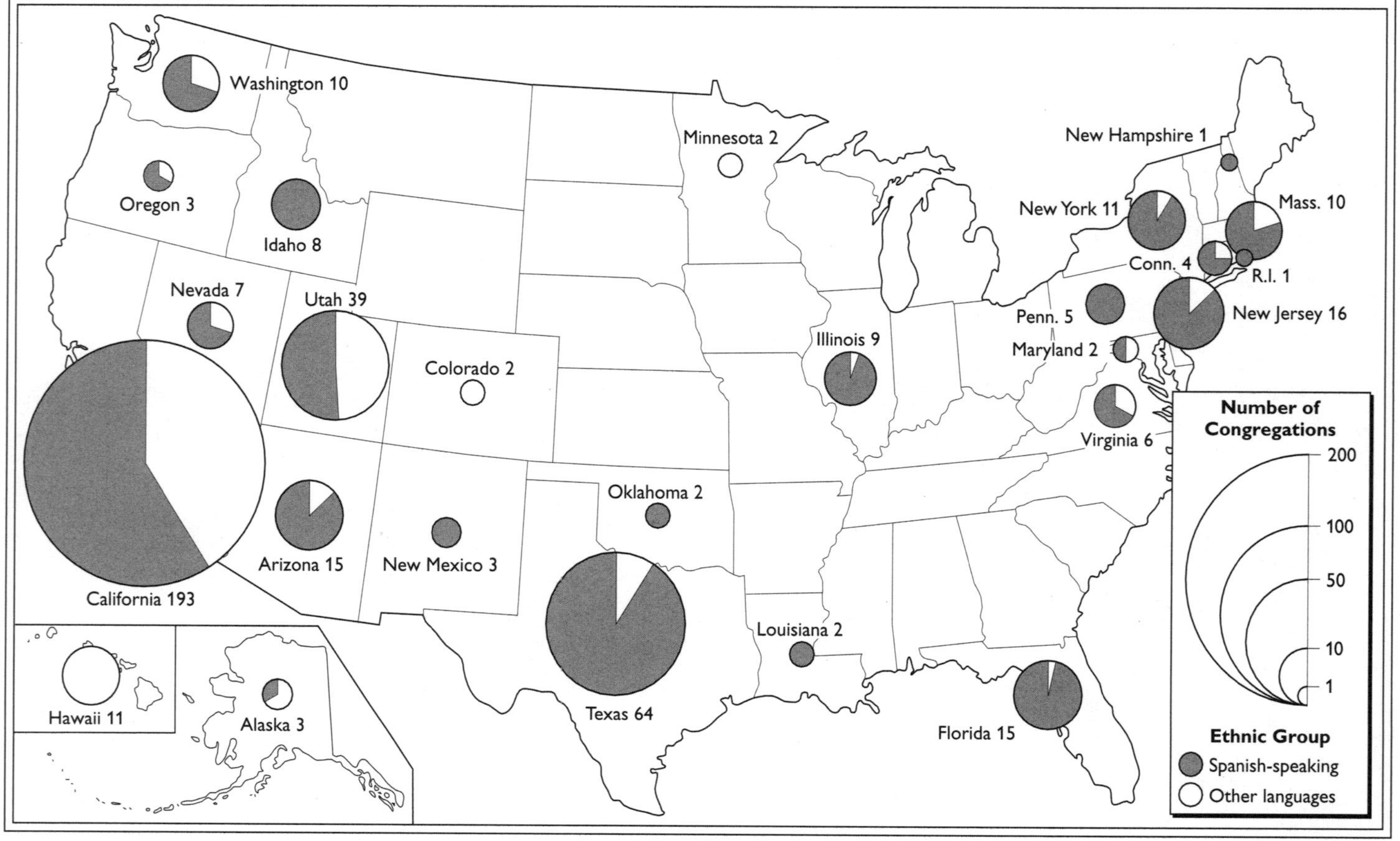

BYU Geography Dept.

area, a Tongan-speaking stake in Salt Lake City, and a largely Navajo stake in Chinle, Arizona.

In 1997 there was talk though of changing the policy again and eliminating these special units. Bishops of Spanish-speaking units in Salt Lake City and Provo, Utah, were told although there were enough wards there would not be a Spanish-speaking stake in those areas. DeAnna Morgan, the wife of the Spanish-speaking branch president in Buhl, Idaho, explained, "The grapevine tells us that non-English speaking branches and wards are being phased out."[21] As I have talked about my research, I have also heard this rumor. Unfortunately, until the General Authorities act, no one will know if these rumors are true or not. And even then the sources will not be available to understand why the LDS Church leaders made the change.

In the meantime, language wards and branches continue in the United States. How the Redd Center interviewees responded to these branches is the subject of the next chapters.

Notes

1. Spencer W. Kimball Journal, 29 July 1964, in private possession. Used by permission of the family.

2. Golden Buchanan, Oral History, interviewed by William G. Hartley, 1975, 5:24, LDS Church Archives, Historical Department, Church of Jesus Christ of Latter-day Saints, Salt Lake City, Utah. (Hereinafter cited as LDS Church Archives.)

3. Kimball Journal, 3 February 1966.

4. "Texas Mission Divided," *Church News,* 16 December 1967, 13.

5. Chad M. Orton, *More Faith than Fear: The Los Angeles Stake Story* (Salt Lake City: Bookcraft, 1987), 288–289; John K. Edmunds, Oral History, interviewed by Gordon Irving, 1980, 82, 87, 137, LDS Church Archives.

6. Grant M. Burbidge, Oral History, interviewed by Gordon Irving, 1973, 58, LDS Church Archives.

7. Leland and McNone Perry, Oral History, interviewed by Gordon Irving, 1972, 71, LDS Church Archives.

8. Harold Israel Bowman, Oral History, interviewed by Gordon Irving, 1973, 76–77, LDS Church Archives.

9. "Boundaries of Three Missions in Southwestern U.S: Realigned," *Church News,* 11 November 1972, 4.

10. Orton, 289.

11. Daniel K. Robins, Oral History, interviewed by Gordon Irving, 1973, 12–13, 66, LDS Church Archives.

12. Conversation with Michael Landon by author, 30 May 1996.

13. Richard L. Jensen, "Mother Tongue: Use of Non-English Languages in the Church of Jesus Christ of Latter-day Saints in the United States, 1850–1983," *New Views of Mormon History: A Collection of Essays in Honor of Leonard J. Arrington,* Davis Bitton and Maureen Ursenbach Beecher, eds. (Salt Lake City: University of Utah Press, 1987), 293.

14. Jessie L. Embry, "Ethnic Groups and the LDS Church," *Dialogue: A Journal of Mormon Thought* 25 (Winter 1992): 83–84; Buchanan, Oral History, 1975, 5, 11, 13; Eduardo Balderas Oral History, interviewed by Gordon Irving, 1973, 75, LDS Church Archives.

15. Buchanan, Oral History, 1975, 5, 11, 13.

16. Enoc Q. Flores, Oral History, interviewed by Emeralda Meraz, 1991, 6–7, LDS Hispanic Oral History Project, Charles Redd Center for Western Studies, Manuscript Division, Harold B. Lee Library, Brigham Young University, Provo, Utah.

17. Buchanan, Oral History, 1975, 5:140; Stewart Durrant, Oral History, interviewed by Richard Jensen, 1973, 19, LDS Church Archives.

18. Durrant, Oral History, 5–6; "Aid Minorities, President Kimball Asks Leaders," *Church News,* 11 October 1980, 4.

19. Durrant, Oral History, 34-35.

20. Flores, Oral History, 7.

21. DeAnna Morgan, letter to author, 19 February 1997.

CHAPTER FIVE

LDS HISPANIC AMERICAN ORAL HISTORY PROJECT

As mentioned earlier, the Charles Redd Center interviewed ninety-four Latino American Mormons about their experiences in the Church. While this was not a representative sample, nearly all the interviewees talked about their experiences in and reactions to Spanish-speaking congregations in the United States. To better understand their reactions, this chapter will profile the interviewees.

Nationality

Interviewees came from twelve Latin American countries plus second-generation Hispanic Americans. Of the ninety-four interviewees, twenty-seven came from Mexico and fourteen from Peru. This distribution reflected Mexican American Esmeralda Meraz's and Peruvian Katuska Serrano's personal acquaintance networks. Serrano conducted most of the interviews with Peruvians. All three interviewers, however, conducted interviews with Mexicans because of the large number of immigrants from that country. Thirteen interviewees were the second generation in the United States.

TABLE 1.
Latino American Interviewees by Nationality

COUNTRY	NUMBER	PERCENTAGE	COUNTRY	NUMBER	PERCENTAGE
Mexico	27	28.7	Puerto Rico	4	4.3
Peru	14	14.9	Spain	2	2.1
United States—second generation	13	13.8	Nicaragua	2	2.1
Argentina	11	11.7	Cuba	1	1.1
Guatemala	8	8.5	Honduras	1	1.1
El Salvador	5	5.3	Brazil	1	1.1
Ecuador	5	5.3	TOTAL	94	100.0

The thirteen who were born in the United States were only the second generation; their parents had immigrated. Most of their parents were from Mexico (eight). Other parents came from Panama (one), Chile (one), Ecuador (one), Guatemala (one), and Argentina (one).

Age and Gender

Forty-four interviewees were men and forty-nine were women. They ranged in age from late teens to over eighty, although nearly half (41) were in their twenties, probably reflecting the bias for BYU students and young adults in the Provo area. Fifty-two of the interviewees lived in Provo, and thirty-four of those were BYU students.

Previous Religious Experiences

Not surprisingly, two-thirds of the interviewees were Catholics before they became Mormons and religion had been very important to about half.

Stella Maria Abraham Vallota, who came to the United States from Argentina as a young married woman in her early twenties in 1969, recalled, "Religion had a prevalent part in my life as I was growing up. I went through all the precepts within the Catholic Church which are baptism, confirmation, and first communion. Those were important stepping stones in my life."[1] Vallota later divorced, went back to school, and then remarried. During that time, religious values changed for her. Pilar Herrera, who was born in Venezuela and grew up in Spain, explained, "I think that our culture and religion go together. If you throw one part of that away and you come up with it missing, it is really hard. . . . Our culture is really old, especially in Mexico and South America."[2]

The other half said religion had not been important before their LDS conversion. Though Herrera described how culture and Catholicism were interwoven in Latin America, that did not happen in her family. "My parents are Catholic but just because they were born in that religion in Spain. They really are nothing. They don't believe in anything. They believe in God in their way. . . . That is how I was raised. I didn't go to church. I didn't believe in the Catholic priests."[3]

Dioni Morales, who grew up in Puerto Rico, said her family was "supposed to be Catholics, but we hardly went to church at all. Probably we went only once or twice a year. When I stayed with my grandma, she made me go. I didn't like it, but I had to. I didn't want her to feel bad. I took some catechism, religion classes. I was baptized a Catholic when I was little.

Then I went through communion when I was eight."[4] Her family joined the Mormon Church in 1982 when she was eleven.

One-quarter of the interviewees grew up in the LDS Church, either because they were born to Mormon parents or because their parents were baptized when the children were young. Enrique Cortez, from Mexico, lived with his grandmother because his parents were divorced and his mother later emigrated to the United States. Cortez's grandmother joined the LDS Church the year he was born, so he grew up attending Primary and youth activities. He viewed the Church as "my mom and father because if it wasn't for the Church guidance, I would have so much stress."[5]

Juan Luis Garcia was born in Peru in 1968 to Mormon parents. His memories of growing up were "church. . . . We went to church every week." He enjoyed the Young Men activities, especially the camp outs. But he did not like family home evening because it was the same "talent show" every week. His belief also did not come easy. "The hardest part was to gain a testimony." When he was fifteen, "I was wondering what I was really doing [at church], I talked to my parents. They said if I wanted to know for sure that the Church was true or not I had to read and I had to pray. . . . Once I read and prayed everything was okay."[6]

Family Life

Fifty-five of the interviewees' parents were together; in twenty-two cases the parents were divorced or separated. Forty said they had at least some family activities; twenty-six said they hardly ever did things as families. Many interviewees had started families of their own. Of the eighty-three where marital status could be determined, fifty-three were married, one was divorced, and thirty had never married. Thirty-eight had one or more children.

Arlene Fuentes, a native of Puerto Rico, was very close to her parents and two younger sisters. When her father worked for Eastern Airlines, they traveled throughout the United States including Disney World, Disneyland, and Hawaii. Although she had little contact with grandparents on either side, she liked her mother's sisters and enjoyed spending time with them.

When the Catholic school she attended in Puerto Rico was going to be closed, her parents searched vainly for a new school, then moved to Texas where there were better educational opportunities. While there, Fuentes made Mormon friends, became interested in the LDS Church, and was baptized at eighteen.

Fuentes met her husband-to-be, a Chilean, when they were both serving in the Chile-Osorno Mission. After their releases, they married, lived in

Chile for a while, moved to Texas, and then came to Provo so her husband could attend Brigham Young University. At the time of the interview, Fuentes had four children and was the Relief Society president in a Spanish-speaking ward in Provo. Although her parents have not joined the LDS Church, they have moved to Provo to be close to her and their grandchildren. Fuentes planned many activities with them.[7]

Ricardo Diaz, a BYU student, grew up in Chihuahua City, Mexico, where "Grandma took care of feeding us, clothing us, and making sure that we were ready for school. She had rheumatism, so she had to stay in the house quite a bit." Because the children spent most the time playing outside, the whole family was together only at bedtime.

In 1974 Diaz, then twelve, moved to the United States with his mother, an inactive Mormon. Shortly after the move, missionaries found them in Silver City, Nevada, taught Diaz and his siblings, and the children joined the LDS Church. His mother remarried a non-Mormon and later divorced him. Diaz was not close to his stepfather. Instead a local Mormon befriended Diaz and helped him feel attached to the Church.

After graduating from high school, he started wondering, "Is this Church really what they say it is?" He decided to attend BYU because it was "far away," but his motive was to discover whether "I am brain-washed, or . . . what the truth is really about the Mormons." After a religion professor encouraged him to study other religions, he read books but did not find answers. He also read the Book of Mormon and New Testament. By the end of the semester, "I was convinced. I can say that by that December I was converted. I don't know at what particular moment it happened, but I know it happened through reading the Book Mormon and the reading of the New Testament together. I could tell that one didn't contradict the other."

This made a difference in how he viewed his family. When he went home, "I realized that I did miss my mom. That was the first time I hugged her and cried when I came back. Our family hasn't been a very touching family. For me to cry and to just feel so hurt because I was coming to leave them again was all related to families, the Church, the Book of Mormon, and the New Testament."[8]

Economics

Because the interviews did not include explicit questions on economic status, it was impossible to determine the financial level of most families.

Forty-two interviewees identified their fathers' occupation: eighteen were in professional positions and eleven were in agricultural jobs. Twenty-seven listed their mothers' occupations: eleven were homemakers. Because the interviewees were young, only twenty-nine listed jobs in their home countries before coming to the United States: eight had been in professional occupations, five were in service industries, four were in agriculture, three were in sales, and three were in clerical positions. In the United States, thirty-four were students and nine were professionals. Others were homemakers (five), laborers (five), and technicians (five).

The coders determined educational level for eighty-eight of the interviewees. Forty-eight had attended some college, ten had baccalaureate degrees, and nine had some graduate studies. Of the rest, eleven had graduated from high school, five had some high school, and five had only elementary schooling. These figures are atypical of especially Mexican Americans. According to a 1991 U.S. Census estimate, just over 50 percent of U.S. residents of Mexican origin thirty-five years of age and older had completed high school. Only 7.4 percent had four years of college.[9] Comparison of these educational figures and occupations shows that the interviewees are more educated and have better paying jobs than most Mexican Americans. So while their insights are helpful, they are not a representative sample of Mexican Americans.

Some examples show the economic conditions of the interviewees. Myriam Lopez Furrows was born in Puerto Rico where her father worked as a painter and her mother was a homemaker. Her older brothers and sisters moved to the United States and then convinced her parents to bring the rest of the eight children to New York. Her father had a hard time finding a job there because he did not speak English.

Myriam's family joined the LDS Church in 1964 when she was eight years old. She graduated from high school and Ricks College, then worked while her husband-to-be served a mission. After their marriage, they moved several times as he looked for work. This economic instability put some stress on the marriage, but she remained a homemaker.[10]

Alfredo Jose Sarrazin grew up in Ecuador where his father taught high school. Alfredo attended several colleges but lost interest quickly. Although neither he nor his parents were Mormons, they sent him to BYU when he was out of high school because they liked the standards. He joined the LDS Church there and was studying engineering when he was interviewed.[11]

Conversion

The readers determined that seventy-eight of the interviewees were converts to the Mormon Church. Others were lifetime members. Forty-seven of the converts first learned about the Church in their native countries. Thirty-one had their first contact in the United States.

How did these converts first learn about the Mormon Church? Information was available on only sixty-eight interviewees. Two-thirds (forty-six) talked to church members. The largest group (twenty-eight) talked to family members. Fifteen talked to friends, and five discussed the Church with members that they did not know very well. The rest (twenty-six) discussed the Mormon Church with missionaries. Nearly all the interviewees were young when they joined the Church. Readers determined the age the interviewees joined for seventy-two cases. Of these, twenty-three joined at the same time as parents or other families members when they were very young. Twenty-seven became Mormons before they were twenty years old. Of the remaining twenty-two, sixteen joined in their twenties, one in his thirties, three in their forties, and only two were over fifty.

While the interviewees' conversion stories often had common elements, each was unique. The decision to change religion and lifestyle required thought and prayer. Some made the decision quickly. Others took more time to decide. Some examples show the variety of experiences.

Joaquin Arcia, a farmer in Nicaragua, was in his forties when he joined the LDS Church, but he had had many questions about religion. After studying the Bible, he did not feel the Catholic religion followed its teachings and contended, "If a judge has a code of procedure that he isn't following, he is committing an illegal act." For two years he "withdrew from all religion." Then, "I knelt down by the side of my bed . . . and said to God, 'Enlighten me to tell me which church is the true church, because I don't want to go through life changing religions.'"

His daughter Amparito, who was newly married, had joined the LDS Church but had not told him. She introduced him to the missionaries. When he learned about the Book of Mormon, he decided, "If this book agrees with the Bible, I'll believe it." Arcia felt that the messages matched, so he became a Latter-day Saint. He summarized his experiences, "I used to say, 'Oh this life is so sad.' But now I know the Gospel, I give thanks . . . that I left that great error." At the time of his interview, Arcia was living in Southern California near a daughter. The Church hired him to help build a church.[12]

Zenon Lara joined the Church in Mexico as a grandfather. He grew up as a Catholic, then joined the Baptist Church when he was dating his future wife. A son-in-law who was a Mormon invited him to listen to the missionaries. Lara and his wife took the missionary discussions and then started going to church. He felt the elders very tactfully convinced him that coffee was not healthy. When his wife stopped buying beer, he stopped drinking. Once he read the Book of Mormon and Joseph Smith's story, he explained, "We . . . thought that only something from God could have translated this book. It couldn't be any other way. . . . This book is so marvelous that he brought us." When he was interviewed, Lara lived in California, attended a Spanish-speaking ward, and spoke very little English.[13]

Hector Ovando grew up in Guatemala in an inactive Catholic family. When he was twenty-nine, he started dating a nineteen-year-old Mormon girl, Sheny. Her family was not happy with the relationship, but her mother invited him to church. He accepted because he was anxious to spend more time with Sheny. "I liked it more and more because it was a peaceful atmosphere, not like the atmosphere I was accustomed to." He took the missionary lessons, but he felt he could not accept the Joseph Smith story. However, he agreed to baptism because of pressure from Sheny's mother. Then "the night before my baptism, I had a dream that I will never forget. . . . It was very real. Someone came and told me, 'Listen, what you are doing tomorrow is the right thing. This is the Church of Jesus Christ. This is the true church. Get baptized.' I woke up the day of my baptism with the real feeling that yes, I had done a good thing. I felt something special when I was baptized." His family felt he only joined "for the girl," but he married Sheny, remained active, and was attending a Spanish-speaking ward in Los Angeles when he was interviewed.[14]

Delmy Mena, a six-year-old Catholic in El Salvador, had neighbors who wanted to share the gospel with her family. They sent missionaries, and Mena's parents were impressed. Delmy remembered going to Primary with the missionaries. However, because her parents were not married, they could not be baptized. When the missionaries had to leave El Salvador in 1977, her parents, who had been very attached to the missionaries, lost interest in attending church. When the missionaries returned, they contacted the Mena family, but the parents did not feel the same closeness to the new Mormon representatives. As a result, Mena and her brothers and sisters also had no contact with the Church. Later her brother decided to return to Church, and Delmy went with him. They became friends with Church members and joined the Church.

Mena met her husband-to-be when the missionaries brought him to a Church activity. Eventually he was baptized. Mena dated him for five years before they were married. They decided to immigrate to Southern California because of the unsettled economic conditions in El Salvador. At first it was difficult to find work because Mena did not receive a work permit until shortly before she was interviewed in 1991. She still struggled with English, and the interview was in Spanish.[15]

Raquel De Luna was born in the United States around 1930 to Mexican parents who returned to Mexico when she was four. Her parents were members, and she grew up in the Church but did not join until she was fourteen. Even then she wondered if she believed. Despite her doubts as a teenager, she decided to go on a mission. After intensive study and prayer, she believed what she was teaching others. She met her husband in Mexico, and they were married in 1959 in the Mesa Temple. De Luna was living in Southern California and attending a Spanish-speaking branch when she was interviewed.[16]

William Linares was also living in Southern California when he was interviewed. Born in 1963 in Peru, Linares attended the LDS Church in Peru when he was a teenager. He recalled, "I was like an active nonmember. I knew quite a few things about the Church, but I guess because I was so young I never decided to make the final step. My mom was the same way." His mother and grandmother emigrated to the United States a few years later; then Linares came. "One afternoon probably two months after I arrived, my mom and I were just talking. We said, 'Why don't we get in contact with the Church again?' " Linares checked the yellow pages and "found one church close to our house which was a . . . ward in Spanish in the Glendale Stake. We decided to call them."

The elders arrived in two days. They retaught the family, and Linares, his mother, and his younger brothers were baptized. Later Linares baptized his grandmother. When asked why he joined the Church, Linares responded, "Somehow I guess I knew a long time ago that the Church was true. I knew it deep inside, but I guess I didn't want to make a commitment with God. Somehow when you are in a strange land and you don't know anybody, it has an effect on you. It is kind of hard to describe. When you are alone, there is nobody else but God. I knew the truth, so I guess the time was right."[17]

Miguel Vargas, an immigrant from Mexico, came to the United States in 1982 as an adult. He felt that he was not really a Catholic and started reading books from other churches. One day he noticed a Book of Mormon in his home and started reading it. He asked some members about it, but they gave him very little information. A long time after that the missionaries visited. At first he hid from them and made excuses not to go to church. But he somehow felt an obligation to the missionaries and agreed to be baptized, hoping that they would leave him alone afterwards. His wife was baptized a month later but also did not attend church. Vargas did not go to church for three months after his baptism. Missionaries returned a year and a half later and invited the couple to church. He lied, saying that he had to work. Finally a member came and accompanied him and his wife to church. They had been steady participants for the ten years preceding the interview in Southern California. At the time he was working construction, but his goal was to become a dental technician.[18]

Ivan Sanchez, a BYU student, was born in Guatemala City and came to the United States with his parents in 1965 at age three. Sanchez suffered from asthma, and a doctor recommended the move. He came with his mother; a year later his father and sister followed. Over the years, the family lived in Indiana, Texas, and Idaho where they joined the Church. Although he was active, Sanchez described himself as not having a testimony until he went on a Spanish-speaking mission in Southern California. He explained, "I was eight when I was baptized. I lived a normal Mormon life until I was nineteen. Then I went on my mission. On my mission is where I got converted—teaching people about the gospel and at the same time learning it myself. . . . I was converted right there in the mission field along with the people that I was converting."[19]

Summary

The Charles Redd Center LDS Hispanic American Oral History Project was created to better understand the experiences of Latinos in the American Mormon Church. While the interviewees are not a representative sample, their honest responses to open-ended questions can illuminate their experiences as Mormons. They openly talked about the strengths and weaknesses of Spanish-speaking congregations, for example.

Notes

1. Stella Maria Abraham Vallota, Oral History, interviewed by Andrea Van Wagenen, 1991, 1, LDS Hispanic American Oral History Project, Charles Redd Center for Western Studies, Manuscript Division, Harold B. Lee Library, Brigham Young University, Provo, Utah. (All the interviews cited in this chapter are from the LDS Hispanic American Oral History Project.)

2. Pilar Herrera, Oral History, interviewed by Andrea Van Wagenen, 1991, 6.

3. Ibid., 1.

4. Dioni Morales, Oral History, interviewed by Andrea Van Wagenen, 1992, 1–2.

5. Enrique Cortez, Oral History, interviewed by Katuska Serrano, 1991, 1, 5.

6. Juan Luis Garcia, Oral History, interviewed by Katuska Serrano, 1991, 2–4.

7. Arlene Fuentes, Oral History, interviewed by Andrea Van Wagenen, 1992, 1–3, 6–7, 22.

8. Ricardo Diaz, Oral History, interviewed by Esmeralda Meraz, 1991, 1, 6, 9–10, 13.

9. Allan Englekirk and Marguerite Marin, "Mexican Americans," *Gale Encyclopedia of Multicultural America*, Rudolph J. Vecoli, ed. (New York: Gale Research Inc., 1995), 921.

10. Myriam Lopez Furrows, Oral History, interviewed by Katuska Serrano, 1991, 1–2, 10, 12–13, 22.

11. Alfredo Jose Sarrazin, Oral History, interviewed by Katuska Serrano, 1991, 1–4, 9.

12. Joaquin Arcia, Oral History, interviewed by Katuska Serrano, 1991, 9.

13. Zenon Lara, Oral History, interviewed by Katuska Serrano, 1991, 4.

14. Hector Ovando, Oral History, interviewed by Katuska Serrano, 1992, 3.

15. Delmy Mena, Oral History, interviewed by Katuska Serrano, 1991, 1–12.

16. Raquel De Luna, Oral History, interviewed by Katuska Serrano, 1991, 1–2.

17. William Linares, Oral History, interviewed by Katuska Serrano, 1991, 4.

18. Miguel Vargas, Oral History, interviewed by Katuska Serrano, 1991, 1–3.

19. Ivan Sanchez, Oral History, interviewed by Katuska Serrano, 1991, 14.

CHAPTER SIX

ADVANTAGES OF ETHNIC WARDS AND BRANCHES FOR ORAL HISTORY PARTICIPANTS

Introduction

Most of the interviewees who participated in the LDS Hispanic Oral History Project attended Spanish branches or wards. In the seventy-nine cases where branch/ward makeup could be determined, fifty-five (70 percent) attended ethnic congregations. Because the Spanish-speaking immigrants came from throughout Mexico, Latin America, and other Spanish-speaking areas, most attended units with members from many countries (64 percent or thirty-nine of sixty-one where branch/ward makeup could be determined). And 67 percent (forty-five of sixty-seven where views could be determined) reported positive experiences. Only five said that they had negative feelings about ethnic congregations; seventeen said they had mixed reactions.

George I. Monsivais, a Mexican American and a research analyst for the Research Division of the Correlation Department of the LDS Church, listed some reasons LDS Latino Americans preferred separate congregations:

- to hear the gospel in the language of their hearts;
- to participate in classes, meetings, and callings without embarrassment or concern over English language ability;
- for children to see their Spanish-speaking parents participate in classes and meetings and function in callings in their wards and stakes;
- to receive training in the language in which they are most comfortable;
- to have interviews conducted without the need of a translator; and
- to have Church-centered associations with individuals who share a common language and cultural heritage.[1]

The Redd Center interviewees confirmed several of these views.

Language

The overwhelming motivation for attending the ethnic wards/branches was language. Some interviewees could not communicate in English. Others spoke some English but not enough to function in a geographical ward.

These people understood the messages in the Spanish congregations. They also participated in the services by offering prayers, giving talks, and answering questions in classes. Even if the interviewees spoke English, they felt more comfortable worshipping in their native tongue.

Mexican American and BYU student Esmeralda Meraz explained language was the major reason her parents attended a Spanish-speaking branch in Southern California. "Though my dad speaks English, he has not mastered the English language and he can't communicate very well. . . . My mom has had less schooling than he has" and could say only a few words in English.[2]

BYU student Burton A. Rojas, a Mexican American who was born in 1971 and grew up in Turlock, California, agreed that language was essential. "I think there are eleven languages in our stake. . . . It is because in America you have the melting pot. It takes a few years for people to really assimilate into the mainstream of society. Sometimes they never do it. I think that it is really important for them to have the opportunity to go to church, take the sacrament, and understand what is being said."[3]

Another BYU student, Mario Valencia, a Mexican American who was born in Texas in 1967, explained, "Sunday is a time to meet with somebody that they have a lot more in common with. . . . They can meet with people that can speak their language. I don't see what difference it would make if you learned the gospel in Spanish or in English."[4]

Miguel Vargas, a first generation immigrant from Mexico, enjoyed his Spanish-speaking ward in Southern California because "everything in our ward is in our language, the messages, the literature, the programs. If it was an English-speaking ward, it would be more difficult for me to understand it. I don't think I would feel comfortable."[5]

Sharing the same language also increased a feeling of group identification. Consuelo Ramirez, a native of El Salvador, enjoyed her Spanish-speaking ward in Van Nuys, California, because "there exists a warmth among brothers, which I believe is very important."[6] Thirty-seven-year-old Marse Cetina, a Cuban living in Los Angeles, California, said, "When we sing the hymns, you can feel in Spanish because of your language. You can feel the spirit. You can really sing with all of your lungs."[7]

Without Spanish-speaking congregations, some members became inactive. Josie Abaroa, a BYU student who was born in San Diego to Mexican parents, recalled that, when her family joined the Church, her father became involved in a Spanish branch. Later when Church leaders decided to combine the wards, her father and about 50 percent of the Spanish unit stopped attending. Abaroa suspected that language was the major reason for their disaffection because the branch helped people like her father learn the gospel. "Even if they go to church and they listen in English, they are not going to understand everything."[8]

Roberto Ayerdis, who was born in 1952, lived in New York just after the 1964 World Fair when many Hispanic Americans joined the Church. His family, inactive converts, started going to Church again because they met the Mormons at the fair. His father even served as a bishop in a Spanish-speaking ward. But the ward was split in the 1970s, and his family was assigned to an English-speaking ward. While Ayerdis's family remained active, "a lot of the [Spanish community] dropped out. Those that were proficient in English have remained, but some of the others have fallen away."[9]

Rosalinda Meraz, a Mexican American living in El Centro, California, and interviewer Esmeralda Meraz's mother, said some members left the Spanish-speaking branch to go to an English-speaking ward but frequently returned within a year. They told her that "they haven't progressed because they don't understand. . . . They say that they don't feel comfortable, that they feel the Spirit more in the Spanish branch. But I believe that the Spirit they feel is because they understand everything that is spoken there."[10]

Ricardo Diaz, an immigrant from Mexico and a BYU student, explained his mother's problems attending an integrated ward in Las Cruces, New Mexico. The ward provided a Spanish Sunday School class, but it was an investigators' Principles of the Gospel class, not the regular Gospel Doctrine lessons. As a single mother, she also felt isolated from families as if she were "an appendage to the Church." Diaz continued that this situation not only made his mother uncomfortable but slowed missionary efforts among nonmember Latino Americans in Las Cruces.[11]

Some Hispanic members attending English-speaking wards may still feel "inactive" because they are not as involved. A woman from Ecuador who was interviewed by the BYU Linguistic Department's Distance Learning Project recalled, "I used to be a leader in my country. . . . I used to the president of the Young Women and the Gospel Doctrine teacher. When I came here [to the United States] I couldn't speak the language, and for me, it was a little bit like I was inactive."[12]

Culture

But language was not the only reason for having ethnic congregations. According to Samuel Victor Miera, who served as president of the Cumorah

Branch in Midvale, Utah, from 1967 to 1971, understanding the language was "just the tip of the iceberg." If the people stayed in the United States long enough, "eventually you don't have to worry about the language because you could work it so it'd all be in English." Problems under the surface included obeying the commandments, especially the Word of Wisdom. Working together and sharing common concerns helped overcome temptations.

As another example of cultural difference according to Miera was socializing. Choir practice, for example, was not a one-hour session on Sundays as in most American English-speaking wards. Instead the choir met Tuesday and Friday. Members sang for forty-five minutes and then visited for three hours.[13] Many Hispanic members also liked to chat before and after church meetings. In most English-speaking wards in the United States, members arrive just before or just after the services have started and leave five minutes after they are over. According to Mexican American Enoc Q. Flores, a BYU employee and former Spanish-speaking bishop, "If you don't understand the [Anglo-American] culture, that is very rude and very antisocial. Americans are business like. They really like to take care of business and go. They go to church. They have been to church, so they can go home. In Latin America you have to stay for three hours and chat afterwards."[14]

Several years ago a Redd Center secretary, Olga de la Rosa, a Guatemalan native in her late twenties, explained that her ward, as part of ward conference, had an activity planned for every night of the week. That night they were having a ward family home evening with a choir in which she would be singing. All were to be dressed in white. In contrast, ward conferences in English-speaking wards in the United States usually mean visits and talks by the stake presidency and auxiliary leaders during Sunday meetings only.

Some interviewees also noted differences in how Anglo American and Hispanic cultures express friendship. Lidia Quiroz, a BYU student who was born in Peru but moved to California as a teenager, enjoyed the Peruvian custom of a kiss of greeting among ward members.[15] Marse Cetina agreed, "In the Spanish ward we see each other, and we embrace each other. Sometimes we give those noisy kisses. Americans don't do that."[16] Nestor Cifuentes, a twenty-seven-year-old native of Argentina who had also lived in Peru, lamented that the custom could not spread Church-wide. "I would like to see among the members of the Church in this country a better expression, a better communication of those feelings about love, as we do in Latin America. We are not only shaking hands, but also we hug, we kiss. I really like this. I really would like to see my American brothers say hi to each other with a kiss as we do as Latins in some parts of Argentina. The scriptures say that. I would say to them, 'Here is what the scriptures say. Say hi to everybody in the Church with a kiss.' "[17]

Victor Rodriguez, who joined the LDS Church in 1960 when he was eight years old in Guatemala, said that members of his Spanish-speaking ward greeted visitors—members and investigators alike—with a hug. Even if they did not join the Church, the members kept in touch. But such affection was unknown in or out of Church with Anglo Americans. "The outsiders all the time complain about the American culture. They are cold. Even if you live next door they never talk to you." Then he lamented, "That is the way it is. There is not much we can do about it."[18]

Gustavo Giuria was born in 1965 in Peru and was living in California when he was interviewed He saw additional differences between Latino and Anglo American culture. "Maybe we are people that are a little more expressive, maybe noisier."[19] Nestor Cifuentes expressed the same concerns, "One of the things that I would really like to share and to even see in the LDS Church is more spontaneity and sensitivity. In Latin America as the members of the Church, we try to share as much of our love and feelings as we can to the others." He continued, "We always say, the American people, even the members of the Church, are cold people compared with us. They are even colder than Argentineans, and much, much colder than Peruvians and Brazilians."[20] Other interviewees talked about how Anglo Americans seem very independent while Latinos willingly worked together. Luis Espinoza, who was born in 1966 in the United States to Chilean parents, commented, "Hispanics flock together. They will actually help each other."[21]

Aspects of culture that made members feel more comfortable involved food, dances, and other socials. For the Spanish American Mission branches, tamale sales and ward parties were important. The Lucero Ward's annual "Piñata Party" drew people from throughout the Salt Lake Valley, and its operettas helped fund-raising in other wards. Besides raising money, the annual December "party of Mexican food, excellent talent, and social dancing has served to provide a much desired contact with Latin culture." The Los Angeles Spanish Branch also held annual fiestas that attracted people from throughout the area.[22]

A strong motivation underlying all of the cultural consideration was simply a desire to be with people who had similar backgrounds, experiences, and understandings. Imelda Lom, a BYU student originally from Mexico, decided to attend a Spanish ward after going to an English-speaking BYU unit "because it had been so long since I have been back to church for the sacrament meeting in Spanish. It feels nice to be with your people." Elizabeth Valdivieso, a convert from Guatemala, used the same phrase of belonging in describing her Hispanic congregation in Van Nuys, California: "They are your people. . . . If you work, you work with your people.[23] Joaquin Arcia, an immigrant from Nicaragua who lived in Glendale, California, described his branch as "family. We all speak as friends, with love. We try to serve one another when there is the need to serve someone."[24]

Anglo American Leslie O. Brewer who worked with a Spanish-speaking branch in Tucson, Arizona, communicated the same concept from his cultural point of view, "There's a type of Mexican person who gets along with Anglos and there's another type that doesn't feel socially adjusted to them."[25] Lyman Sidney Shreeve, who served as a branch president in Mesa, Arizona, from 1938 to 1945, agreed. He said most of the Spanish-speaking people stayed in the branch even if they spoke English because "they felt more comfortable there than in the wards."[26] Former branch president and regional representative in 1974 Arturo Martinez summarized, "I think there are certain aspects of our culture that are good, that will contribute, that certainly make our lives more colorful, both spiritually and otherwise."[27]

Some interviewees feared that these cultural elements might be lost, submerged by "traditional Mormon culture" in an integrated ward. As Francisco Guajardo, a twenty-seven-year-old native of Mexico attending BYU, explained, "We should teach the people that they can still maintain a lot of their traditions, a lot of their holidays, and they don't need to give these things up." He then used Relief Society examples to show the differences he saw in culture. "I don't see why all Relief Societies should make quilts and can. They don't need to do that in a place where it's hot and vegetables are plentiful all year round."[28]

Perceived Prejudice

Some Hispanic Americans felt uncomfortable in English-speaking wards because they perceived that the members did not accept Spanish speakers. Frequently such situations involved not properly decoding cultural signals. Monsivais described a possible situation. An English-speaking American member might walk past a group of Latino Americans whose ward meets in the same building. Reasoning that the group is absorbed in an enjoyable conversation and not speaking Spanish, the English speaker does not address them. A group of Anglo Americans would probably accept such behavior as normal, even courteous; but in many Hispanic cultures, it would be considered insulting.[29]

Samuel Victor Miera explained a similar concern. When members of the Cumorah Branch went to geographical wards, they often complained that English-speaking members would not speak to them or sit by them in church. Miera added he had also had similar experiences where he felt "ignored" which was "the most frustrating thing," even more than outright prejudice.[30]

Nineteen-year-old Martha Zavala, a BYU student who had lived most of her life in the United States, agreed. When she lived in New York, there were many Latinos, and everyone would say, "'How are you?' Give them a little kiss and a hug. It is the most common thing." But that did not happen in Provo even in her apartment. "Sometimes here my roommates would walk in the door and they would not even say hello. At first I was taking it personally, but then I realized that that is just the way they are. They are just drier as opposed to Latins who are just warm and very affectionate and expressive."[31]

Stella Maria Abraham Vallota, an Argentine immigrant and psychologist in Southern California, discussed some of these concerns. When she attended the San Marino English-speaking ward, members "were doing all the nonverbal behaviors when they were talking with us like raising their voices, opening up their eyes, and acting as if 'are you understanding what I'm saying?' " She said that since she spoke with an accent people assumed that she was from "somewhere," but after dealing with her, they would realize "I am an American citizen now, and I know all the functions of how the society works . . . perhaps more than somebody who was born here and never learned about that."[32] Her daughter, Andrea Van Wagenen, felt that her mother and stepfather had problems in the San Marino English-speaking ward. "My parents felt like they weren't quite appreciated. . . . Their heritage wasn't appreciated; their language wasn't appreciated."[33]

Some interviewees also disliked the European Americans assumptions that all Spanish-speaking members are the same. Enoc Q. Flores, who was born in 1943 and grew up in the Mormon colonies in Mexico, worked for the multicultural office at BYU. He explained, "A lot of people don't know the difference between Mexico, Chile, Peru, Argentina, and Brazil. They are very, very different. Many of them don't even know where the countries are. When they speak, sometimes they make a lot of mistakes. They are ignorant mistakes. But they offend other people from down there."[34]

Imelda Lom, a twenty-year-old Mexican attending BYU, agreed, pointing out that some European American Mormons needed to get "rid of the stereotypes. For example, most Americans think that Latin Americans are lazy, they don't like to work, or they are dirty. I think that we need to get rid of the negative stereotypes and get to know the people for what they are as individuals."[35]

Gloria Moreno, interviewer Esmeralda Meraz's aunt, moved from Mexico to Watsonville, Northern California. She joined the Church after her sister Rosalinda Meraz and had enjoyed attending Mormon services in Mexico and in Southern California with her sister. But she felt members of the English-speaking ward "didn't invite" her to participate. She became inactive and started attending the Catholic church where she "began to feel like I used to feel at home" despite a nagging "emptiness." When she did muster the courage to attend the English-speaking ward, she felt that the members treated her like a visitor.[36]

Teresa Andrade, who was born in Mexico in 1944 and joined the Church in the United States, attended a Spanish-speaking branch in Southern California. She sensed that "some of the brothers and sisters of English-speaking wards are prejudiced. . . . Sometimes you can feel it. As an intelligent person that I think I should be, I know the fact and keep going. If we have any kind of prejudice against one another it is because we lack some kind of knowledge. When that happens, I just ignore it. But some people, to my regret, don't ignore it. Some people don't like to go and meet with English-speaking." She felt that there had been a lot of prejudice when she joined in 1978 but was pleased that "now the young people are erasing that," adding, "They are living together. They are communicating. They are friends. They are calling on the phone. They are learning about their cultures."[37]

Anglo American Lyman Sidney Shreeve described one unusual case of perceived prejudice in the 1970s. In Aurora, Illinois, the Spanish-speaking members helped build a meetinghouse, met with an integrated ward, and then they had their own Sunday School class. However, many Spanish-speaking people stopped attending when the Church leaders had their class meet in the hall because there were not enough classrooms. Shreeve argued the English-speaking people who were less concerned about the hall-implied message of marginalization could have met there, but the leaders did not recognize the cultural reactions.[38]

Ana Maritza Landaverde, a forty-seven year old immigrant from El Salvador, felt less racism in California than in other places. Members of the Church treated her well and tried to get to know her despite the language barrier. They helped her with translation and stake callings. Still she complained that some people had stereotypes and felt the Latinos did not keep the church buildings clean.[39]

Teresa Andrade, an immigrant from Mexico who joined the LDS Church in California, took a broad intercultural view of discrimination. "Some of the brothers and sisters of English-speaking wards are prejudiced," she conceded. Sometimes you can feel it." She added, "When I try to look at this the other way around, we have been prejudiced, too, as Mexicans, or as minorities. We have been prejudiced because we don't want to mingle with them. We don't want to follow their example. We criticize their ways."[40]

Bricia Zoraya Rodriguez, a BYU student who grew up in the Los Angeles area where her family had moved from Mexico, felt that she had problems sometimes because she did not always know how to relate to English-speaking Americans just as they did not know how to relate to her. Attending predominantly Anglo wards as a child and teenager, she "felt a little alienated sometimes. People were friendly, but I don't think a lot of white people know how to deal with differences." As a result, she was "a little bit shyer toward" Americans. "I felt really self conscious about what I was doing and what I was saying." She clung to other Hispanic people "that were caught in the same situation that I was."

She agreed with Andrade that the "alienation" was not one sided. "I probably alienated myself as much as they alienated me. They didn't as readily approach me as they would another white person." She continued, "More in my heart I kind of did feel rejected because of my ethnicity. I did feel discriminated against. I am not trying to rationalize it, but I think a lot of it was due to their ignorance." For example, since she was Mexican, European Americans assumed she could not speak English.[41]

Callings

A major source of fulfillment for Spanish-speaking members in ethnic wards was their ability to receive church positions and participate completely in church programs. Having a lay ministry dependent on volunteers in local congregations sets the Mormon Church apart from many other religions. Catholic sociologist Thomas F. O'Dea observed, "The church provided a job for everyone to do, and perhaps more important, has provided a formal context in which it is to be done. The result is a wide distribution of activity, responsibility, and prestige."[42]

In the BYU Linguistics Department survey, half of whom who were Spanish speakers, 47.8 percent felt "at church, native and nonnative English speakers have the same opportunities for callings." But those high figures might be because many respondents attended non-English-speaking congregations.[43]

Redd Center interviewees who had been in both situations, however, felt the ethnic congregations gave them greater chances to serve. When asked how she would feel if she had to attend a geographical ward, Mexican American Teresa Andrade responded, "If it had to be English? It would jeopardize my growing. Being a member of a ward that is Spanish-speaking, I can teach. I can learn from whatever sources there are to learn and teach them with the Spirit. As you can see, in English, people would be very bored to hear me. Probably the opportunities won't be there for me in leadership positions that can make me grow. I have been the Primary president and Relief Society president. I have been a teacher. Right now I am the chairman of the activities committee. I don't remember how many callings I have held, but it never would have been possible if it would have been in English. My growth and some other people's growth would have been jeopardized."[44]

Esmeralda Meraz's parents had the same experience. Her father served as branch president in a Spanish-speaking unit in El Centro, California. When his job forced him to travel more, he became Sunday School president. Her mother Rosalinda had "probably pretty much done about everything. She has worked in the Primary. . . . She has been Relief Society president before. She was the Young Women's president."[45] When asked how she would feel if there were no Spanish-speaking branch, Rosalinda Meraz pleaded, "Please don't make me go to the English ward." She continued, "I think it would be a step backward for me. I like to be helping, working in the Church."[46]

Rosalinda's sister, Gloria Moreno, was inactive because she did not feel needed in the ward. "I think in the Church to be active, to feel committed, to enjoy it and learn more, and not let things get lukewarm, you've got to be involved in the activities and have responsibilities in the Church. If you don't have responsibilities in the Church, you can't stay active. I think that is what happened to me."[47]

When the Spanish branch in New York was reorganized in the 1970s, Roberto Ayerdis's mother was reluctant to accept a calling in the geographical ward. When asked to be the chorister, she asked, "What do I know about leading songs in English?"[48]

Arturo Martinez described a Spanish-speaking member in Salt Lake Valley, a Brother de la Cruz, who had the same feelings when the Cumorah Branch was dissolved in 1974. In the Spanish branch he was the high priest group leader and helped the branch send in more family group sheets to the Genealogical Society than any ward in the stake. When he went to the English-speaking ward, he did not have a calling. While some Cumorah members were doing well in 1975, the Lamanite and Minority Committee figured that for 40 percent "progress had just come to a complete stop."[49]

Feelings if Branch/Ward Were Dissolved

Redd Center interviewees were often asked how they would feel if the Church leaders discontinued the Spanish-speaking ward/branch they attended and asked them to go to a geographical ward. Almost all responded negatively. As forty-two-year-old Cristina Jenks, who immigrated to California from Argentina in her twenties and was married to a European American, explained, "The way we are growing, I think that is very far from reality because it is very large." Then she added, "I would hate to see that ward dissolved. These people won't have a place to go and worship the Lord because most of them don't speak English. There are only a few of us. They will probably learn, but they would rather attend a Spanish-speaking unit than English, and I understand why."[50]

While Jenks spoke about other people, some interviewees gave personal reasons. Alfredo Sarrazin, a twenty-six-year-old convert from Ecuador living in Provo, went to a Spanish ward because he had "many friends. . . . I pretty much know everyone there." He felt if he went to the English-speaking ward he would not "know anybody. . . . I probably would not enjoy it as much as I do right now."[51] Marco Valdivieso, a forty-one-year-old Peruvian living in California, agreed that the ward provided friendships. As a member of the bishopric, he said, "I know the members" and their concerns. "We love the people." He added thoughtfully, "I think I can change my mind. I think very fast. . . . We need to multiply the Church and divide."[52]

Others agreed that they would go to a geographical ward but it would not be their first choice. Angela Cabrera, a thirty-three-year-old Peruvian living in California in 1991, felt, "I wouldn't like [going to a geographical ward] but I would do it if I had to." She added that the advantages would be "I would have to meet new people which is nice." She believed "we would share the same principles and values. There would be no problem."[53]

Summary

George I. Monsivais summarized the reasons he felt the Church had ethnic congregations. "Those who decry the creation of minority-language units only on the basis of cultural protectionism . . . have likely misunderstood the issue, just as much as those who espouse creating and attending Spanish-language units as a way to reinforce Hispanic culture and teach Spanish to their children. Church is not about learning the language of men but rather learning to commune with God. Providing gospel opportunities in different languages should have this as its end."[54] Nearly all the Redd Center interviewees agreed. And while some pointed out some problems in language branches, others felt the same issues strengthened the branches and wards or were not issues. Some of these concerns will be discussed in the next chapter.

Notes

1. George I Monsivais, "Our Respective Lands of Jershon," *"For Ye Are All One in Christ Jesus:" The Global Church in a World of Ethnic Diversity* (Provo, UT: David M. Kennedy Center for International Studies, Brigham Young University, 1996), 51.

2. Esmeralda Meraz, Oral History, interviewed by Jessie Embry, 1991, 5, LDS Hispanic Oral History Project, Charles Redd Center for Western Studies, Manuscript Division, Harold B. Lee Library, Brigham Young University, Provo, Utah. (Unless otherwise cited, interviews cited in this chapter are from the LDS Hispanic American Oral History Project.)

3. Burton A. Rojas, Oral History, interviewed by Esmeralda Meraz, 1991, 12.

4. Mario Valencia, Oral History, interviewed by Esmeralda Meraz, 1991, 5.

5. Miguel Vargas, Oral History, interviewed by Katuska Serrano, 1991, 9.

6. Consuelo Ramirez, Oral History, interviewed by Katuska Serrano, 1991, 12.

7. Marse Cetina, Oral History, interviewed by Katuska Serrano, 1991, 12.

8. Josie Abaroa, Oral History, interviewed by Andrea Van Wagenen, 1991, 5.

9. Roberto Ayerdis, Oral History, interviewed by Janean Baker, 1992, 17–18.

10. Rosalinda Meraz, Oral History, interviewed by Esmeralda Meraz, 1991, 9.

11. Ricardo Diaz, Oral History, interviewed by Esmeralda Meraz, 1991, 26–27.

12. Dena Marie Wright Erickson, "The Relationship Between Non-Native English Speakers' English Proficiency and Their Callings in the LDS Church in the United States" (M.A. thesis, Brigham Young University, 1995), 4.

13. Samuel Victor Miera, Oral History, interviewed by Gordon Irving, 1975–76, 65, LDS Church Archives, Historical Department, Church of Jesus Christ of Latter-day Saints, Salt Lake City, Utah. (Hereinafter cited as LDS Church Archives.)

14. Enoc Q. Flores, Oral History, interviewed by Esmeralda Meraz, 1991, 14.

15. Lidia Quiroz, Oral History, interviewed by Katuska Serrano, 1991, 10–11.

16. Marse Cetina, Oral History, 8.

17. Nestor Cifuentes, Oral History, interviewed by Andrea Van Wagenen, 1991, 12.

18. Victor Rodriguez, Oral History, interviewed by Andrea Van Wagenen, 1991, 5.

19. Gustavo Giuria, Oral History, interviewed by Kataska Serrano, 1991, 18.

20. Cifuentes, Oral History, 9.

21. Luis Espinoza, Oral History, interviewed by Andrea Van Wagenen, 1992, 12.

22. Lucero Ward, Manuscript History, 6 December 1958, LDS Church Archives; Chad Orton, *More Faith than Fear: The Los Angeles Stake Story* (Salt Lake City: Bookcraft, 1987), 301.

23. Imelda Lom, Oral History, interviewed by Andrea Van Wagenen, 1992, 4; Elizabeth Valdiveso, Oral History, Katuska Serrano, 1991, 5–6.

24. Joaquin Arcia, Oral History, interviewed by Katuska Serrano, 1991, 10.

25. Leslie O. and Nina Brewer, Oral History, interviewed by Ronald K. Esplin, 1973, 18, LDS Church Archives.

26. Lyman Sidney and Afton K Shreeve, Oral History, Gordon Irving, 1974–75, 35, LDS Church Archives.

27. Arturo R. Martinez, Oral History, interviewed by Gordon Irving, 1975, 264, LDS Church Archives.

28. Francisco Guajardo, Oral History, interviewed by Andrea Van Wagenen, 1991, 6–7.

29. Monsivais, "Our Respective Lands of Jershon," 52.

30. Miera, Oral History, 65.

31. Martha Zavala, Oral History, interviewed by Katuska Serrano, 1991, 14.

32. Stella Maria Abraham Vallota, Oral History, interviewed by Andrea Van Wagenen, 1991, 6.

33. Andrea Van Wagenen, Oral History, interviewed by Jessie Embry, 1991, 8.

34. Enoc Q. Flores, Oral History, interviewed by Esmeralda Meraz, 1991, 9.

35. Lom, Oral History, 3.

36. Gloria Moreno, Oral History, interviewed by Esmeralda Meraz, 1991,

37. Teresa Andrade, Oral History, interviewed by Katuska Serrano, 1991, 24–25.

38. Shreeve, Oral History, 40.

39. Maritza Landaverde, Oral History, interviewed by Katuska Serrano, 1991, 12.

40. Andrade, Oral History, 24, 29–30.

41. Bricia Zoraya Rodriguez, Oral History, interviewed by Andrea Van Wagenen, 1991, 6–7.

42. Thomas F. O'Dea, *The Mormons* (Chicago: University of Chicago, 1957), 184.

43. Cheryl Ann White, "Factors in the Lives of LDS Church Members that Promote and Inhibit the Acquisition of English as a Second Language" (M.A. thesis, BYU, 1995), 44.

44. Andrade, Oral History, 18.

45. Esmeralda Meraz, Oral History, 6.

46. Rosalinda Meraz, Oral History, 5.

47. Moreno, Oral History, 5.

48. Ayerdis, Oral History, 18.

49. Martinez, Oral History, 263.

50. Cristina Jenks, Oral History, interviewed by Katuska Serrano, 1991, 8–9.

51. Alfredo Sarrazin, Oral History, interviewed by Katuska Serrano, 1991, 19.

52. Marco Valdivieso, Oral History, interviewed by Katuska Serrano, 1991, 10–11.

53. Angela Cabrera, Oral History, interviewed by Katuska Serrano, 1991, 5.

54. Monsivais, "Our Respective Lands of Jershon," 54.

C H A P T E R   S E V E N

SOME PERCEIVED PROBLEMS WITH U.S. SPANISH-SPEAKING BRANCHES/WARDS

Introduction

A few of those who attend Spanish-speaking congregations saw problems. Others who attended English-speaking meetings wondered if Spanish-speaking units helped or hindered members. Some interviewees felt that many Latinos in the United States were not learning the culture or language well enough to cope successfully and that separate congregations increased that problem. Other Redd Center informants looked at the various cultures represented in the Spanish-speaking branches and felt there was too much diversity for such units to remain viable. Finally, some wondered what would happen to new generations growing up with English as their primary language outside the home. Could the Spanish-speaking congregations meet their needs? As always, it was evident that no perfect solution existed. Meeting the needs of one group left another group ill served or neglected.

Not Learning Culture or Language

Some interviewees wanted to learn English and American culture and felt that attending an ethnic congregation did not provide that opportunity. Thirty-three-year-old Lorenza Zamarron, who grew up in Mexico and was attending BYU, said she had enjoyed attending a Spanish-speaking branch in Texas but decided to attend a English-speaking congregation instead of one of the Spanish wards in Provo when she "realized that my English was not progressing." She summed up her position: "You don't improve your English and do not learn the culture of this country. With that you are not able to interact with a different society. You must learn about the society. It is your responsibility even though you may feel that they are discriminating against you. Even if they do, it is your responsibility to overcome that and show them that you are able to progress." Although she felt she spoke English like a four-year-old, she felt that she should attend the English-speaking ward.[1] Patricia Serrano, a Peruvian who joined the LDS church at age fifty-five in California, agreed. She explained in Spanish, "I think that for me one of the disadvantages would be not practicing my English."[2]

Various Countries and Cultures Represented

The Hispanic American Mormons had mixed reactions about the policy that grouped all Spanish speakers in the same branch. For some, it was not a concern or was an obstacle quickly overcome. Marse Cetina, a Cuban native living in Los Angeles, California, explained when asked if there were national groups in her ward, "I think it is natural. Sisters from Salvador like to be with sisters from Salvador. I don't know anyone from Cuba, so I am all by myself all over there. But I love all of them. They are so special, each one of them. I have my own blood sisters, but I think I love more my spiritual sisters than my own sisters. Everyone is teaching me something, and everyone is so patient with me because I talk too much. They never say, 'Marse, shut up.' I am learning so much from them. When I have a problem and I call them or they sometimes call me, it makes me feel like God is sending them to me with special guidance and a special message."[3]

Juan Luis Gracia was born in Peru in 1968 to Mormon parents and was attending BYU in 1991. He felt that the various nationalities should "mingle and know about each other."[4] Rebecca Arciniega, a BYU student from Mexico who attended Spanish-speaking wards at Ricks and BYU, agreed. "Even though there were people from different Latin American countries, we really didn't care about countries. We just cared about each other as friends."[5]

Arlene Fuentes, a native of Puerto Rico in her thirties, had lived in Chile, Texas, and Provo. Most members of her Provo Spanish-speaking ward were Mexicans and they seemed to "prevail" at activities. While some said that the Mexicans were clannish, she disagreed. They were just strong in the things that they had in common. Despite different foods and even a different language for those from Brazil, "it seems like the Latin American in them is the same everywhere. I don't see very much difference."[6]

The differences were not only nationalities. Cristina Jenks, an immigrant from Argentina who came in her early twenties, had attended a small Spanish-speaking branch in Bakersfield, California, shortly after she came to the United States and just after she was married. The branch had members from a different economic background than Jenks was accustomed to.

"The people were all field workers and had very little education." Yet "it was fun. But it was a lot different from what I was used to."[7]

Forty-one-year-old store supervisor Marco Valdivieso in Southern California felt, "In the United States when I attend a Spanish branch or ward, there are a lot of people coming here from different countries. The members are not very mature spiritually. So I can recognize a difference. I think in South America the members are stronger." But he added that he liked to go to the branch because "the subject of the Church is to serve one another."[8]

But some interviewees felt that the national mix detracted from their worship. Argentinean Ines Calderwood, a twenty-six-year-old office worker in Provo, said, "I have always loved Latins because I am one." But differences could easily become discrimination. "For example, Mexicans really think that Mexico is the greatest. I don't know if it is because they are in North America and we are in South America. . . . The Argentines . . . think they are the best because we are more European. It is okay. We are. Maybe we dress better than Peruvians because Peruvians are more Indian. But I know great people from Peru. Probably they are not pretty. But you don't have to be pretty to be nice."[9]

Another twenty-six-year-old, Gustavo Giuria, a native of Peru who had attended Spanish-speaking units in New York and California and worked in an auto parts store, acknowledged, "It was different for me because it was my first time with different kinds of people in the same place, people from Colombia, Peru, Venezuela, Puerto Rico, and whatever place. The way that they talk is different. The way that they think is different. It took me three or four months to get involved with the Church like I was in Peru. The people in New York were picky. They were looking for what you are doing and looking over you. It was different. I have to adapt to the Church, not the Church to me."[10]

Interviewer Andrea Van Wagenen, originally from Argentina, felt she got along fine with Mexicans, but she had noticed some prejudice between other Argentines and Mexicans. "The Argentineans tend to think that they're superior because their Spanish is different and because they're more European in their mannerisms. Of course, Mexican people are very proud of their heritage, as they should be."[11]

BYU graduate student Marcelo Gigena, also from Argentina, came to the United States with his family as a child. He commented on "one upmanship" in the Spanish-speaking wards; people from different countries liked to correct each other and "Latins are very proud. . . . In most of these Spanish wards there could be ten countries represented in one ward.

You could have an Argentine, a Chilean, a guy from Ecuador, a guy from Peru, and then another. There's a multiplicity of ideas that can go from these people. . . . Often they would like to say, 'No, brother, it is this way.' They like to correct each other or else they like to outdo each other in faith, in spirit, or in something."[12]

European American Daniel Robins, who served a mission to Northern California in the early 1970s, recalled problems between Mexicans and Chileans. Each thought that the other group spoke poor Spanish. He recalled a time when a Chilean was speaking in sacrament meeting and a Mexican complained that he could not understand the Chilean.[13]

Possible Segegration

Having separate congregations meant that Spanish-speaking Mormons did not interact very often with English-speaking members. Most respondents did not see this as segregation. In the Cumorah Branch, according to former President Samuel Victor Miera, branch members enjoyed meeting together because they felt it preserved some of their identity. They did not want to assimilate. "They just wanted to be themselves and be accepted for who they were and what they were, and not try to lose their identity, but just be regular, normal members of the Church."

Miera continued, "We don't want to separate ourselves, but we don't want to be mainstreamed either." He continued that Americans had not accepted Mexicans as they had Northern Europeans; consequently, Mexicans "stick longer with our traditions and our language and our customs and our culture." While he hoped that society would integrate Mexicans, he added, "I guess it just probably takes forever until a person can feel free and at ease and fully accepted."[14]

While most interviewees seemed to agree with this view, one, Steven Chris Vigil, a BYU student in his twenties who grew up in Colorado, interpreted segregated branches as discrimination within the Church. "I believe that by having these wards established here in Utah it is a way for the Church to suppress the minority people. Let me tell you why. I believe that the best way to build relations in the Church is for people to intermingle with one another. However, when you have an Oriental branch, a white branch, a Lamanite branch, or a Hispanic branch, you begin to segregate people into specific areas. You don't allow them to intermingle and share the culture which is necessary."[15]

Twenty-one-year-old Norman Garcia, who grew up in the United States and was attending BYU, approached the lack of interaction from another view. He feared that Spanish-speaking members "would feel isolated. Only Spanish-speaking people would go to the Spanish activities. They wouldn't have a General Conference type of atmosphere. They probably wouldn't like stake activities. They probably would think that they couldn't fit in as well. Probably they would say, 'I only know Spanish. I can't talk to other people.' "[16]

Organizational Concerns

Because ethnic branches were often small, they sometimes lacked the entire Church program and lacked leadership. In 1996 and 1997, approximately two-thirds of the Spanish-speaking congregations in the United States were branches and not wards. The wards were usually in California, Utah, Texas, and Florida, the areas where, with the exception of Utah, there were also enough Spanish-speaking members for a stake. The number of branches shows the types of organizational problems. A branch organization is usually not only smaller but does not have enough priesthood leaders to operate as a ward.

Esmeralda Meraz went from a fully functionally ward in Mexico to a Spanish-speaking branch in California. "It was kind of discouraging to see only ten people . . . in the meetings. It was also discouraging not to see any youth. We [she and her three sisters and one brother] were the only kids that were attending church." It was difficult to operate Primary and Young Women's. Meraz continued, "We always had a feeling of not being complete and of not having everyone there that needed to be there to make it a successful experience for us every Sunday."[17]

Arturo Martinez, a former branch leader and regional representative in Salt Lake City, wanted his children to learn to speak Spanish—a benefit of attending an ethnic ward—but he also recognized that the smaller unit could not sponsor a Boy Scout unit like the geographical ward.[18] Twenty-year-old Burton A. Rojas, a Mexican American who served a Spanish-speaking mission in California, agreed. "I saw a lot of Spanish branches that haven't really come into their own yet. There are not enough members."[19]

Other interviewees felt English-speaking branches had more structure. William Linares, a twenty-eight-year-old native of Peru, attended a geographical ward and explained, "It is more organized than the Spanish ward was. I am not saying anything about the Spanish ward. What I am saying is that they are more organized because most of the people have been members all of their lives. In the Spanish ward, most of them are just newly converted, so they need a lot of help getting things organized."[20]

Mexican American Esperanza Silvas-Ayerdis agreed. Born in 1952 in Texas, she joined the Church in England when she was in the military through the influence of her "sweetheart" who became her husband. They had lived in California, Panama, and Washington, D.C., by the time she was interviewed in 1991. She recalled serving as a Relief Society president in a Spanish-speaking branch in California shortly after she joined the Church. Her husband, Roberto Ayerdis, was branch president at the same time. She recalled, "It was kind of hard, but Lamanites are good people. They have a spirit that engulfs you. They want to serve, but they are not used to serving. It is hard for them to get in the habit of preparing their lessons. I would come to church one Sunday, and my spiritual living teacher had not prepared. She would say, 'I didn't prepare,' and she would sit there. I was trying to train them and trying to do my calling and their callings."[21]

Pavel Ramos, a convert from Guatemala who had served a mission and was attending BYU in 1991, said this misunderstanding led to additional problems. As an elders quorum president in a Spanish-speaking ward in Provo, he saw "home teaching is way low. When we ask for service projects, few people show up." He complained, "If we can't do our home teaching or we can't go help someone like a widow to paint her house or something, how are we going to show that to someone who doesn't know?"[22]

When the Spanish-speaking branch was small, frequently there were not enough leaders. Cristina Jenks's branch in Bakersfield had ten people. When she was interviewed in 1991, she was attending a very large Spanish-speaking ward in Glendale, California. She enjoyed her current situation but had mixed feelings about the small branch. "We have great leaders [here]. In some of the small branches they don't, and sometimes it is disappointing because things are not done the way they should be done."[23] Esmeralda Meraz agreed. Her small branch in Southern California "didn't have the leaders. It didn't have people that were strong in the gospel."[24] Lack of leadership is frequently a concern in any small LDS branch, so these concerns are not unique to Spanish-speaking members in the United States.

While Hispanic Americans worshipped and served in congregations in their native language in the United States, only a few belonged to Spanish-speaking stakes. The rest had to work with English-speaking leaders. So while technically any ward/branch member could serve in a stake leadership position, these callings often went only to English-speaking members or to Spanish-speaking members who spoke both languages. As one bishop explained, Spanish-speaking members "can [have callings as] Sunday School teachers, Relief Society teachers, Gospel Essentials teachers of Spanish class, but . . . having them for Elder's Quorum or High Priest Group Leaders, or counselors to bishops . . . is very hard" because they could not communicate with stake leaders.[25]

Several Spanish-speaking members discussed the struggles they had in stake meetings. Maria Lepe Nelson recalled that shortly after she joined the Church in the 1970s the bishop asked her to work with the Young Women. "The hardest part for me was to go to the meetings on the stake level. I did, but I understood only 10 percent of the meeting because my main language was Spanish at the time." Still, she kept attending, struggling to understand what was going on.[26] Forty-seven-year-old Teresa Andrade also "didn't know what they were talking about" in stake Primary meetings when she began attending. But she continued to go and "learned a lot from reading the books of the Church in English and listening to their talks."[27] One woman from the BYU Linguistics Department study said that she always took a daughter or granddaughter to interpret for her at stake Primary meetings. That way "there is always someone. . . by my side who helps me."[28]

Second Generation

Another problem that time forces on even very successful Spanish-speaking wards is how to deal with youth who grow up in the United States, not speaking Spanish. This is, of course, not a unique LDS problem. One of the fastest growing Protestant churches in the world, the Seventh Day Adventist Church now has 8 million members worldwide with about three-quarters of them living in the United States. Latinos constitute the fastest-growing segment of this church's ethnic converts in the United States. Most of them are first generation immigrants. According to Ron Crane, a professor at a Seventh Day Adventist university, "Highly acculturated Latino Adventist youth" are less likely to maintain distinctive Adventist standards: no dances, jewelry, or movies. As a result, acculturation "threatens the viability of . . . the strong boundaries that define the identity of a community of faith."[29]

Mormons also express a variety of concerns of how to relate to the second generation. When one woman interviewed for the BYU study was called to teach teenagers in Sunday School, she was delighted but added, "I struggle . . . to explain things to them and they cannot explain it to me and . . . we get stuck halfway. . . . Since they are in school . . . and speak only English, they hardly speak Spanish or they don't want to. . . . They will read . . . to me in English; they can explain it in English, but they cannot explain it in Spanish."[30]

Rebecca E. Arciniega, a BYU employee from Mexico City, explained that a bishop in a Spanish ward in Provo "wanted the classes for the Primary children to be taught in English which I was against. I thought that since it was a Spanish ward that everything should be in Spanish." She added that things might have changed since more Spanish-speaking people also speak English.[31]

Noemí Lombardo, a forty-three-year-old from Argentina, explained the same problem from her children's point of view. After pointing out that English had become her children's first language, she added, "I never forced them to learn how to read or write in Spanish." However, in their Spanish-speaking ward in Van Nuys, California, some teachers "didn't like them to read . . . from their English scriptures" and "treated my children like, 'Don't you like to speak your native language?' " For a while she considered going to an English-speaking ward to avoid the problem, but her children have chosen to read and write Spanish on their own.[32]

When some Church programs are in English, parents are also frustrated because they cannot help. Teresa Andrade recalled wanting to help her son with the scouting program. Leaders told her to read the Cub Scout manual, but it was in English and she could not understand it. Then her son insisted, "This is for me to read." She continued, "Now I understand why because if I would have read the book I would have made him work on his assignments."[33]

Summary

While most of the Redd Center interviewees enjoyed attending the Spanish-speaking branches, a few identified some disadvantages. Others, however, did not see these concerns as problems. Another way to approach the same concerns is to look at the strengths of integrated units, the subject of the next chapter.

Notes

1. Lorenza Zamarron, Oral History, interviewed by Katuska Serrano, 1991, 11–12, LDS Hispanic American Oral History Project, Charles Redd Center for Western Studies, Manuscript Division, Harold B. Lee Library, Provo, Utah. (Unless otherwise cited, the interviews are from the LDS Hispanic American Oral History Project.)

2. Patricia Serrano, Oral History, interviewed by Katuska Serrano, 1991, 10.

3. Marse Cetina, Oral History, interviewed by Katuska Serrano, 1991, 9.

4. Juan Luis Garcia, Oral History, interviewed by Katuska Serrano, 1991, 12.

5. Rebecca E. Arciniega, Oral History, interviewed by Katuska Serrano, 1991, 7.

6. Arlene Fuentes, Oral History, interviewed by Andrea Van Wagenen, 1992, 12–13.

7. Cristina Jenks, Oral History, interviewed by Katuska Serrano, 1991, 7–8.

8. Marco Valdivieso, Oral History, Katuska Serrano, 1991, 6, 10.

9. Ines Calderwood, Oral History, interviewed by Andrea Van Wagenen, 1991, 8.

10. Gustavo Giuria, Oral History, interviewed by Katuska Serrano, 1991, 9.

11. Andrea Van Wagenen, Oral History, interviewed by Jessie Embry, 1991, 9.

12. Marcelo Alfredo Gigena, Oral History, interviewed by Katuska Serrano, 1991, 14.

13. Daniel K Robins, Oral History, interviewed by Gordon Irving, 1973, 51, LDS Church Archives, Historical Department, Church of Jesus Christ of Latter-day Saints, Salt Lake City, Utah. (Hereinafter cited as LDS Church Archives.)

14. Samuel Victor Miera, Oral History, interviewed by Gordon Irving, 1975–76, 236, LDS Church Archives.

15. Steven Chris Vigil, Oral History, interviewed by Katuska Serrano, 1991, 13.

16. Norman Garcia, Oral History, interviewed by Katuska Serrano, 1991, 7–8.

17. Esmeralda Meraz, Oral History, interviewed by Jessie Embry, 1991, 5, 10.

18. Arturo R. Martinez, Oral History, interviewed by Gordon Irving, 1975, 263, LDS Church Archives.

19. Burton A. Rojas, Oral History, interviewed by Esmeralda Meraz, 1991, 11–12.

20. William Linares, Oral History, interviewed by Katuska Serrano, 1991, 7.

21. Esperanza Silvas-Ayerdis, Oral History, interviewed by Janean G. Baker, 1992, 10.

22. Pavel Ramos, Oral History, interviewed by Andrea Van Wagenen, 1991, 6–7.

23. Cristina Jenks, Oral History, interviewed by Katuska Serrano, 1991, 7–8.

24. Esmeralda Meraz, Oral History, 5, 10.

25. Dena Marie Wright Erickson, "The Relationship Between Non-Native English Speakers' English Proficiency and Their Callings in the LDS Church in the United States" (M.A. thesis, Brigham Young University, 1995), 50.

26. Maria Lepe Nelson, Oral History, interviewed by Katuska Serrano, 1991, 4.

27. Teresa Andrade, Oral History, interviewed by Katuska Serrano, 1991, 21.

28. Erickson, "The Relationship," 53.

29. Ken R. Crane, "Immigrant Adventists and Sectarian Shift: A Case Study of Latino Adventism," copy in possession of author.

30. Erickson, "The Relationship," 53.

31. Rebecca Arciniega, Oral History, interviewed by Katuska Serrano, 1991, 9.

32. Noemí Lombardo, Oral History, interviewed by Katuska Serrano, 1991, 15–16.

33. Teresa Andrade, Oral History, interviewed by Katuska Serrano, 1991, 22.

CHAPTER EIGHT

VIEWS OF INTEGRATED WARDS

Introduction

Despite the generally positive reaction of Spanish-speaking members to ethnic wards, LDS Anglo American Church leaders on the general and local levels do not see ethnic congregations as the permanent solution. Anglo American Stewart Durrant, who worked on several Church committees including the Indian and Minority Committee, explained in a 1973 interview: "We want to fit these people into the regular units of the church. All these special branches are temporary. . . . We hope that some day we can all sit down together as brothers and sisters in the same meeting and use the same material." While he agreed that Spanish-speaking units helped preserve the language skills that might be lost in the integrated ward, he continued, "We need the strength of the Spanish people and they need our strength. We need to build each other. When we're separated, to a certain extent we lose that strength and that opportunity of being in the midst of other people who have some strength that we ought to incorporate into our lives."[1]

This chapter will examine the pros and cons of integrated wards from the points of view of the interviewees who attended geographical wards and branches in their native countries, scholars who have examined the role of community in building unity and avoiding conflict, interviewees' comments about integrated wards, and policies operative in other churches which provide joint services.

Church Attendance in Native Countries

The forty-five Latter-day Saint interviewees who joined the Church in their native countries before immigrating to the United States talked about attending meetings in their home countries. Most saw no major differences between their congregations and those in the United States. They seemed to agree with the 1993 BYU Linguistic Department study where most respondents (79.1 percent of 617 surveyed agreed or strongly agreed) reported that the Church was the same wherever they had lived. Most in the Linguistic survey (70.7 percent) also agreed or strongly agreed that "going to church in my country feels the same as going to church in the United States."[2] The only differences Noemí Lombardo, a forty-three-year-old convert from Argentina living in Southern California, observed between the Church in the United States and her home country were "the physical things:" air conditioned buildings, lots of books, and good pianos. She continued, "Other than that it is exactly the same."[3]

But other interviewees identified more substantial differences. Some from small branches commented on a lack of closeness in their U.S. congregations. Some in Utah said it was a challenge to be a Mormon minority outside the United States and members had more faith. Adenaver Zambrano, a twenty-six-year-old BYU student from Ecuador, explained, "The environment [there] is different. You get to know more the people in the Church down there than here. I don't know if it is society or the culture that has that influence, but I feel more welcome in the Church there than here." He added, "It is probably the culture. I am more adapted to that one than this."[4]

Edwin Espinel, who was born in 1964 and grew up in Ecuador, also saw cultural differences. As a teenager, he had been a leader in the organization for young men, known then as Mutual, in his home country. "Everybody knew each other. Everybody worked toward something. It was not mainly for personal gain but for everybody's gain. . . . I got along with everybody very well. In fact, I miss it because we were sincere in that sense. I grew up thinking that I could be anybody's friend and I could rely on anybody in my ward. The sad experience happened when I came to the United States. I didn't find that closeness in people. Maybe it is because it is a different culture. I think that we weren't selfish in the things that we did and the things that we believed."[5]

Elena Camargo, who grew up in a small town in Peru but moved to Lima at age seventeen, attributed differences in involvement to the setting rather than the country. "In my hometown I noticed that the people were more open, more giving, more loving, more sensitive to the Spirit. I really liked that a lot. In Lima it seemed people were involved with daily things that they were supposed to do. It is a bigger city. People were not as sensitive to the Spirit because they were too busy thinking of other things." Still she liked either ward in Peru better than those in the United States "because the people are so humble and they are so receptive to the Spirit."[6]

Reasons for Integrated Wards—The Scholarly Research

Scholars have found community plays an important part in people's life. According to evolutionary psychologists, humans need to relate intensively with a limited number of human beings rather than superficially with a large number. While there are disadvantages to living in a small town because everyone knows everyone else's business, it also provides an atmosphere of caring. Evolutionary psychologists John Tooby and Leda Cosmides, for example, believe the television series *Cheers* was so popular because it showed a place where a small group of people met regularly and shared their lives. Reporter Alan Ehrenhalt describes a similar setting in Chicago during the 1950s where "each saloon was a sort of a community center."[7]

But saloons were not the only place where people got together in small groups. According to Ehrenhalt, the Chicago of the 1950s brought people together in many ways. Jobs were limited. People did not have "flex hours"; they took fixed lunch hours; they came and left work at the same time. They shopped at small corner stores where they knew the owners and the owners knew them. After pointing out many of these differences, Ehrenhalt concluded, "It should not be necessary to belabor the question of how all these rituals have changed in the decades since then." As a result, he saw a "longing among millions of Americans now reaching middle age for a sense of community." The dilemma remains: Are people willing to sacrifice the choices available at larger stores, more workplaces, and wider circle of possible friends for the closeness of the small town?[8]

LDS wards and branches provide the type of communities that evolutionary psychologists call for. Small towns in nineteenth-century Utah were often only one ward so the village and the ward had the same boundaries. As the Church expanded beyond the Wasatch Front, wards continued to play an important role in defining community. As historian Douglas D. Alder explained Mormon wards and branches are more than congregations where people meet together to hear a preacher. They bring together people from all walks of life who work together on service projects, staff the ward, pray together, and socialize together. None of the ward leaders is paid. For the ward to function, 150 members must accept responsibilities and perform them on a regular basis. In addition, home teachers (two men) are assigned to visit each family and visiting teachers (two women) are assigned to each woman in the ward. Ward members teach each other, attend church-sponsored parties, and lay bishops and branch presidents counsel members in all aspects of their lives. In the process, all the members learn to interact and form a recognizable group identity.[9]

A geographical ward is about the same size as a small village. Its boundaries let members easily say, "On one side are my people. On the other side are strangers." The members share common acquaintances, values, and history with the people within their boundaries, creating a community. That type of unity can exist in an LDS ward in Lima, Peru, or Provo, Utah.

The same results, even without geographical boundaries, occur with ethnic congregations. Just as Latter-day Saints living outside the Mormon Corridor expand their "village" to include Mormons living fifty miles away because they attend the same branch, Spanish-speaking people in the United States can see those in their congregation as "our people." The English-speaking wards become the strangers.[10]

According to some scholars, this type of separateness, while fostering internal community and providing space for cultural differences, damages understanding of and identification with the larger Mormon community. George I. Monsivais, from the Research Information Division of the LDS Church, listed some conclusions from studies of conflict theory and applied them to LDS wards and branches. These studies point out:

1. "Groups are more competitive than individuals."
2. "Communication between participants increases the amount of cooperative behavior. Communication, however, has a much more positive effect on individuals than groups."
3. "When noise is introduced into a game situation (noise here means cooperative behavior being randomly misrepresented to participants as competitive behavior), the likelihood of a cooperative outcome declines."[11]

Monsivais continued that frequently Spanish-speaking and English-speaking wards compete with each other especially when they share buildings. The units vie to use the building for weekday activities. When there is another language group involved, they also argue over space allowed for that language in the library, space for language hymn books in the chapel, and who decides the length of activities and the times the meeting house is available.[12]

Some examples show the types of concerns Monsivais was referring to. A positive sharing example was the McAllen Spanish-speaking Branch in Texas. During the 1960s the branch had its only chapel, but as membership declined, it became a dependent unit in the district in 1972. Six months later it began sharing the building of the McAllen First Branch to save remodeling and repair costs to the separate building. Anglo American District President Clarence McKasson told the Spanish-speaking members "that we should not feel as members of a second class, but on the contrary, feel better because of the better facilities there. [We should] consider the branch is as much ours as theirs." The minutes which end in December 1972 record the difficulties in finding transportation to the other chapel but also record the cooperative cosponsoring of a Christmas social.[13]

But not all activities in all buildings ran smoothly. The Walnut Creek, California, Spanish-speaking branch shared a building with English-speaking wards and the stake. Communication was not always clear between the various groups. The minutes explain that on 5 December 1959 "a branch Christmas party was sponsored by the Relief Society. The hall was beautifully decorated and the tables arranged in a very artistic manner. The entire branch was in attendance. Gifts were exchanged and Santa Claus was there. However, a conflict in the arrangement dates for clearance of the hall arose and we had to move the party into one of the other rooms so that a Stake MIA dance could be held in the recreation hall."[14]

Without mechanisms for communication and conflict resolution, these contests—such as sharing a building—are generalized as characteristics or stereotypes of the group. English-speaking Americans insist that the Spanish speakers should learn to speak English, therefore requiring less space for library materials. Hispanic members say Anglos are too organized and object to Hispanics being in the building for so long because they are emotionally cold and do not enjoy personal interactions. Anglo Americans unknowingly offend Hispanic Americans by walking by without speaking. Hispanic Americans feel that Anglo Americans treat them as inferior when their Sunday School class, due to crowded conditions, must meet in the hall.[15]

Reasons for Integrated Wards—The Redd Center Interviewees

Some Redd Center interviewees argued for integrated wards on similar grounds of community building. Burton A. Rojas, a twenty-year-old BYU student from Turlock, California, saw intermixing as the best way to understand cultural differences. He felt that lessons and entertainment about a culture would increase mutual sympathy because "people tend to be more critical of something they don't understand."[16]

Forty-one-year-old Marco Valdivieso from Peru explained, "For six months I attended an American ward in Salt Lake City. For one month every Sunday I introduced myself to the same people. They would say, 'Oh, you are a member of the ward?' The next Sunday I was introduced to the same people. They would say, 'Oh, you are a member of the Church?' So they forgot. Then they ignored me." However, "One day I remember I felt the spirit and I expressed my testimony. When I finished, a lot of members, American people came. They were around me. 'Oh congratulations. It was a nice spirit. It was a nice testimony.' I waited for this. I need to push, or I need to talk with the spirit to say, 'Hey, I'm here.' Then they recognize, 'Hello, I am here. I have a testimony, too.'" He became a "Spanish guy . . . [who] knows the gospel."[17] He felt he had achieved understanding by letting English-speaking Americans get to know him.

Sara Ulloa, a twenty-one-year-old BYU student from Peru, also felt more interaction was desirable. "One of the things that bothers me in a way is that sometimes I have known people, not even just Spanish speakers, but like Japanese, and people from Asia, will just get together with their own group, like with their own friends from back home." As a result, they don't make new friends. She affirmed, "The best way to get to know someone is just through activities, playing games, just going up to the canyon or just doing something together, even a dance."[18]

Ines Calderwood, a twenty-six-year-old BYU student from Argentina, suggested that a joint party might help break down barriers. "Maybe there could be an organization that can get people together and force the people to get together and to know each other. The Latin ward is having a party. Americans are not going to go to the party. Why? It is because it is Latin music they don't like or vice versa. Maybe it would be nice to have a party that is Latin and American and invited everyone."[19]

Noemí Lombardo, who grew up in Argentina, agreed. She liked to have callings and to participate in the Spanish branch but wanted to "mingle" with the English-speaking American members. "They keep talking about the Anglos and the Hispanics even inside the Church," she lamented. "Instead of 'We, the members of the Church,' it is 'We, the Spanish, and they, the English.'"[20]

One interviewee felt she got to know Anglo Americans better outside Utah. Arlene Fuentes's family moved from Puerto Rico to Texas where she joined the Mormon Church as a teenager. After a mission and marriage, she moved to Utah. She felt it was harder to be an ethnic member of the Church in Utah than it was in other places. "It seems like outside of Utah people just cling together because they are members of the Church. It doesn't matter if they are Hispanic, black, or whatever. Here the ones that have always lived in Utah stick together, the Hispanics stick together, and everybody has their own groups."[21] Unfortunately, the Redd Center was not able to interview other Latino Americans from Texas and other places where there are sharp conflicts between Mexican Americans and European Americans. According to BYU professor Ignacio Garcia, who has lived in Texas and Arizona, the conflicts in the larger communities often carry over to the LDS Church.[22]

Steven Chris Vigil, who grew up in Colorado, also felt he was not treated as a minority until he came to BYU. His first campus bishop suggested that he attend a ward that was 95 percent Native American. Vigil continued, "The Saints here in Utah are judgmental. I think they are judgmental because they fear the Lamanite people. . . . They are seeing minorities infiltrating a white church. I think that scares them."[23]

Since most of the Redd Center interviewees were living in Utah, they reported that experience. Some, like Vigil, felt some type of prejudice from Anglo Americans living in Utah. Mexican American Imelda Lom, a student at BYU, said American Mormons—especially in Utah—"think they have brought the gospel to us. If it wasn't for them, we couldn't have the gospel." Others talked about ignorance. Mexican American Kenneth Gonzales, another BYU student, explained, "I probably definitely have experienced some racial ignorance. . . . They are just ignorant of what minorities experience and who they are." Mexican American Mario Valencia, also a student, agreed, "I don't have any problems with white LDS people, but I think there is a lot of passive prejudice, a lot of ignorance here in Utah. I don't know about other places. Back home there wasn't in Texas that I have been able to see where they felt they were more chosen than others."[24]

Yet other interviewees felt a closeness with European Americans in Utah. Elena Camargo attended a BYU congregation with "a lot of rich kids." But she added, "Even though they have a lot of money, they are really strong in the Church. . . . They are really nice." At first she felt that "because English is my second language" Church leaders did not give her callings. However, at the time of the interview in 1991 she had just been asked to teach a Gospel Doctrine class in Sunday School.[25]

Despite a lack of the closeness he had felt in Ecuador, Edwin Espinel always attended an English-speaking ward. He went first to learn the language and continued to go even when his mother, who could not speak English, joined him because she "like[d] the people."[26]

Twenty-one-year-old BYU student Marco Diaz from Peru pointed out that not all wards are the same. The first BYU ward he attended was "the best ward in the world. We had three activities per week. We had a whole bunch of things going on. Everyone was so friendly and so open." In the ward he attended in 1991 most of the members were older and "I guess because they have a lot of money everybody does their own thing. The ward is not really united." He continued, "Hopefully I will go to a ward that is really united."[27]

Models of Integration

Catholic Church

Other churches in attempting to integrate Latinos have also tried various solutions. The American Catholic Church, for example, has had to deal with a large minority of Latino Americans since the nineteenth century. While initially the Church provided ethnic congregations for all immigrants "to preserve the religious life of the old country," they backed away from that idea in the mid-twentieth century. As one historian explained, separate parishes "reinforced the ethnic differences of the people and enabled neighbors to build cultural barriers among themselves." In 1980 the National Catholic Council of Bishops "urge[d] all Americans to accept the fact of religious and cultural pluralism" and encouraged the development of parishes "that serve more than one nationality." The bishops argued that segregated parishes had been "ill-conceived [because they] were based on mistaken perceptions of cultural affinities."[28]

As the Catholic Church was moving away from ethnic congregations, Hispanic immigration increased and Latinos complained that their needs were not being met. As a result, the American Catholic Church sponsored National Encounters for Hispanic Catholics in 1971 and again in 1977 where clergy and lay leaders discussed the Church's role in helping the poor and encouraging change. A similar meeting of bishops took place in Chicago in 1980. In 1985 the Catholic Diocese of Salt Lake City sponsored a "Hispanic Encuentro" for Catholics from New Mexico, Arizona, Colorado, and Wyoming. Meetings like these led to the U.S. Catholic bishops publishing a pastoral letter on *The Hispanic Presence: Challenges and Commitment* in 1983. Recognizing that in Hispanic culture "faith and life are inseparable," the letter promoted the Office of Hispanic Ministry's training of priests to work with Spanish-speaking Catholics.[29]

But the problems did not disappear with meetings and letters. Historian Dolores Liptak charged in 1989, "American Catholic leaders were not inclined to recognize the many cultural and spiritual gifts of Hispanic Americans or value their contribution to the American Catholic Church." She argued that only after Catholics started joining other churches did local dioceses establish study groups to examine how to keep the Hispanic members.[30]

In 1994 these concerns continued. In a study on Hispanic Catholic culture, Jesuit Allan Figueroa Deck speculated the Protestant churches were successful because they required informal training for their ministers, provided small congregations where the people lived, appointed ministers from the community and empowered them, and seldom questioned the use of the Spanish language in meetings. He added American Catholic worship allowed more participation than what the Hispanics were used to and their popular folk religion practices were frequently not much different than the Pentecostal. Hispanics often got lost in large parishes.[31]

Historian Jay P. Dolan concluded that since the 1960s the Hispanic Americans had formed almost their own church within the Catholic Church. He continued, "All of us in the Church should broaden the embrace with which we greet our Hispanic brothers and sisters and deepen our commitment to them. If we do not, then it is certain that the number of Hispanic Catholics will dwindle in the years ahead."[32]

The Catholic Church has realized it must deal with Spanish-speaking members. A 1990 survey by the Secretariat for Hispanic Affairs found twelve dioceses with at least 50 percent Hispanic members. Many parishes that had been multicultural were Spanish. Recognizing the need to service these members, 40 percent of the dioceses required future priests to speak Spanish.[33]

To deal with these growing numbers, some ethnic parishes hold all of their masses in Spanish but other parishes are experimenting with different ways of combining worship. Julianna Boerio-Goates, a Catholic chemistry professor at Brigham Young University, attends this second type of parish in Provo—St. Francis. In a 1995 article she explained 60 percent of the parish's families had Hispanic roots. The priest spoke some Spanish and the associate was a native of El Salvador who grew up in Mexico and trained for the seminary in California. The parish held three masses in English and three in Spanish weekly. Both priests performed Spanish and English masses so they could meet the members although the associate priest usually celebrated the Spanish services.

For holidays everyone worshipped together. The centennial of the parish was in both languages. The priests encouraged English-speaking Americans to attend such Spanish culture activities as Las manañitas at the Lady of Guadalupe festivals and Las posadas and luminarias before Midnight Mass at Christmas. Hispanic Americans, in turn, were especially invited to more European American activities such as the parish picnic.[34] So more members could worship together for Christmas Eve mass, the Catholics borrowed the LDS Provo Tabernacle in 1996, the first time the LDS building was used for another church's worship. Several masses in English and Spanish and a midnight mass in both languages was held.

Church of the Savior

The Festival Church in Virginia, one of nine small congregations within the Church of the Savior, provides another interesting model. According to a newspaper article, its people of color complained the meetings were "too white." To resolve the problem, the group decided to celebrate the differences among its four major groups: African Americans, Latinos, Asians, and European Americans. Each group takes charge of services and a dinner after the meeting. There are few Asians, so that week is a potluck dinner. Members feel that "sharing food becomes one of the bridges between us."

The Church of the Savior limits its congregations to thirty people. This deliberately forces everyone to interact with everyone else present. There have been troublesome times. In their services, Hispanics went "with the flow." African Americans continued their meetings until they were "over." European Americans wanted to start and stop on time. Over time "the Hispanics come a little more on time, and the whites are less uptight." The reporter summarized, "Meanwhile, as they work at solutions, members enjoy going to one another homes and traveling together to family events. And an occasional potluck meal with quesadillas, greens and bulkogi, a Korean meat dish, makes the challenges go down a little more sweetly."[35]

LDS Comparisons

Neither solution may work for the LDS Church. Catholic parishes are much larger and do not make the same demands for participation (and resultant closeness) required by an LDS ward where lay members take charge of all activities and having callings is an important badge of membership. On the other hand, a ward is much larger than the Festival Church, and it might not be possible for the ward to be similarly structured.

Book of Mormon Option

LDS researcher George Monsivais used the Book of Mormon to consider another option. When the Anti-Nephi-Lehites were forced to leave their

Lamanite homeland after joining the Nephite church, the Nephites gave them a land of their own, but both groups worked together on the common goal of self-defense. The Anti-Nephi-Lehites had resolved not to use arms, so they planted crops. Their sons, who had not taken the oath, joined the Nephite army.

Monsivais suggested that wards create opportunities for Spanish-speaking and English-speaking members to work together on common goals and that youth, who frequently speak English, be involved in activities outside the Spanish-language communities. While he saw value in continuing ethnic congregations, he also felt that there should be opportunities for Spanish- and English-speaking members to "work together toward common goals while developing individual personal relationships, and practicing charity, patience, and forgiveness."[36]

Monsivais did not list possible projects. That might not be possible since concerns would vary depending on the location, members, and available activities. Ignacio Garcia described some possibilities that he tried as bishop of the Spanish-speaking ward in Tucson, Arizona, in the early 1990s. He told the stake president that the members of his ward would not put on socials where they cooked and presented talent for the stake. However, Garcia explained that the Latinos would participate in socials where all ethnic groups provided food and talents. Under those circumstances, one group would not be "entertaining," but everyone would be sharing. Garcia explained as a result the Spanish-speaking members became more involved in stake activities, something that they had not done before.[37]

Monsivias also suggested that the youth from the Spanish-speaking units could be more involved in activities outside of their branches. However, Ignacio Garcia pointed out such efforts had not always been successful. When he was called as a bishop in Tucson, he looked at the various ways that other wards and stakes were dealing with the youth. In the Mesa, Arizona, area, the stakes were experimenting with combining English- and Spanish-speaking youth activities. After the Spanish-speaking youth attended sacrament meeting with their parents, they went to Primary, Young Women, and priesthood meetings with a English-speaking ward. Garcia did not like this arrangement because he felt that it split the families. While some people argued that the Spanish-speaking wards had trouble serving the needs of teenagers, Garcia explained that his Tucson ward developed a very successful Boy Scout and youth program that others wanted to attend.

Besides the problems of separating the youth from their parents, Garcia also wondered about other concerns. One would be providing physical space. The Mesa wards had large enough buildings where two wards could hold sacrament meeting at the same time and then have classrooms for adult priesthood, Relief Society, and Sunday School classes while the youth meet together. Not many Mormon chapels are built that way. Other concerns would be which language and culture would be stressed. Would the Spanish-speaking youth be expected to fit the English-speaking pattern? Where would the leaders come from? Would they all be English-speaking?

Some Redd Center interviewees also talked about their concerns with combined youth activities. Interviewer Esmeralda Meraz attended a Spanish-speaking branch in El Centro, California, and went to a daily early morning religion class, seminary, with English-speaking students. She complained that the teenagers there "saw me as a different person. . . . They would make remarks and say things that didn't make me feel very good and didn't make me feel like I belonged." She continued she liked going to the branch because "they were not going to make a reference to my skin color or the fact that I am Mexican."[38]

Summary

There are several ways to look at integrated wards. The interviewees talk about their experiences in their native countries and in the United States. Many felt closer to the members in the smaller congregations in their homelands. Part of the reason for that might be because, as evolutionary psychologists have pointed out, humans can relate closely better to smaller groups. The smaller branches they attended before they came to the United States provided more of a sense of community than the larger wards or branches they attended at the time they were interviewed.

As has already been pointed out, Latino American Mormons do not agree on the advantages and disadvantages of having separate language congregations. With the growing number of Latino Americans, some agree with Latino scholars that the Spanish-speaking members need space to be able to assimilate at their rate which will be slower than the nineteenth-century Northern European immigrants. This space can be provided in ethnic congregations. Others, however, enjoy meeting together in integrated wards.

Over the years LDS General Authorities have debated whether separate language congregations or integrated wards work best in the United States. Other churches have faced the same concerns and come up with several models with varying success. Since no one system works perfectly for everyone involved, the programs have frequently been changed. In 1997 LDS Church leaders are once again questioning what works best. Should Latino speaking members who speak English go to geographical wards—an experiment being tried in Tucson? Should there be separate Spanish stakes where the members have almost no contact with English-speaking members? One Spanish-speaking stake appears to be in the process of being dissolved. For a while the wards have been eliminated, leaving only the stake organization intact. The process seems to have been reversed.

What is the best way to approach ethnic congregations? This question applies to all non-English speaking groups in the United States. For some groups, though, there are not enough members for wards or even branches. That is not a concern with Spanish-speaking Mormons in the United States since there are so many Latino members. I will address some of the questions on how to deal with ethnic congregations in the next chapter.

Notes

1. Stewart Durrant, Oral History, interviewed by Richard Jensen, 1973, 9–10, 16, LDS Church Archives, Historical Department, Church of Jesus Christ of Latter-day Saints, Salt Lake City, Utah. (Hereinafter cited as LDS Church Archives.)

2. Cheryl Ann White, "Factors in the Lives of LDS Church Members that Promote and Inhibit the Acquisition of English as a Second Language" (M.A. thesis, Brigham Young University, 1995), 52–53.

3. Noemí Lombardo, Oral History, interviewed by Katuska Serrano, 1991, 10–11, LDS Hispanic American Oral History Project, Charles Redd Center for Western Studies, Manuscript Division, Harold B. Lee Library, Brigham Young University, Provo, Utah. (Hereinafter cited as LDS Hispanic American.)

4. Adenaver Zambrano, Oral History, interviewed by Katuska Serrano, 1991, 8–9, LDS Hispanic American.

5. Edwin Espinel, Oral History, interviewed by Esmeralda Meraz, 1991, 5, LDS Hispanic American.

6. Elena Camargo, Oral History, interviewed by Katuska Serrano, 1991, 7–8, 13–14, LDS Hispanic American.

7. John Tooby and Leda Cosmides quoted in Robert Wright, "The Evolution of Despair," *Time* 146 (28 August 1995): 50–57; Alan Ehrenhalt, *The Lost City: Discovering the Forgotten Virtues of Community in the Chicago of the 1950s* (New York: Basic Books, 1995), 13.

8. Ehrenhalt, *The Lost City*, 13–15, 17, 23.

9. For information on Mormon wards as community see Douglas D. Alder, "The Mormon Ward: Congregation or Community," *Journal of Mormon History* 5 (1978): 61–78 (citations from pages 62, 70). Also see Reba L. Keele, "Is Religious Community an Oxymoron?" *Sunstone* 16 (November 1993): 13–21) and Mario S. De Pillis, "The Persistence of Mormon Community into the 1990s," *Sunstone* 15 (October 1991): 28–49.

10. I thank Ron Shook for sharing these ideas with me.

11. George I Monsivais, "Our Respective Lands of Jershon," *"For Ye Are All One in Christ Jesus:" The Global Church in a World of Ethnic Diversity* (Provo, UT: David M. Kennedy Center for International Studies, Brigham Young University, 1996), 51–52.

12. Ibid., 52.

13. McAllen Spanish Branch Historical Record, 1952–72, LDS Church Archives.

14. Walnut Creek Stake, Mexican Branch, LDS Church Archives.

15. Ibid.

16. Burton A. Rojas, Oral History, interviewed by Esmeralda Meraz, 1991, 17, LDS Hispanic American.

17. Marco Valdivieso, Oral History, interviewed by Katuska Serrano, 1991, 11–12, LDS Hispanic American.

18. Sara Ulloa, Oral History, interviewed by Katuska Serrano, 1991. 19, LDS Hispanic American.

19. Ines Calderwood, Oral History, interviewed by Andrea Van Wagenen, 1991, 11, LDS Hispanic American.

20. Lombardo, Oral History, 11.

21. Arlene Fuentes, Oral History, interviewed by Andrea Van Wagenen, 1992, 16, LDS Hispanic American.

22. Ignacio Garcia, Conversation with the author, 13 March 1997.

23. Steven Chris Vigil, Oral History, interviewed by Katuska Serrano, 1991, 10, LDS Hispanic American.

24. Imelda Lom, Oral History, interviewed by Andrea Van Wagenen, 1992, 3, LDS Hispanic American; Kenneth Gonzales, Oral History, interviewed by Esmeralda Meraz, 1991, 11, LDS Hispanic American; Mario Valencia, Oral History, interviewed by Esmeralda Meraz, 1991, 20–21, LDS Hispanic American.

25. Camargo, Oral History, 13.

26. Espinel, Oral History, 16.

27. Marco Diaz, Oral History, interviewed by Katuska Serrano, 1991, 20, LDS Hispanic American.

28. Jay P. Dolan, *The American Catholic Experience: A History from Colonial Times to the Present* (Garden City, NY: Doubleday and Company, 1985), 164, 207–208, 197, 21, 44; Dolores Liptak, *Immigrants and Their Church* (New York: Macmillan, 1989), 191, 192, 202.

29. Isidro Lucas, *The Browning of America: The Hispanic Revolution in the American Church* (Chicago: Fides/Claretian, 1981), 67–68; *Salt Lake Tribune*, 11 May 1985, D1; 18 May 1985, B13; Juliana Boerio-Goates, "The Catholic Church and Ethnic Diversity: A Historical and Personal Perspective," *"For Ye Are All One in Christ Jesus"*. . . , 18.

30. Liptak, *Immigrants and Their Church*, 189.

31. Allan Figueroa Deck, SJ, "The Challenge of Evangelical/Pentecostal Christianity to Hispanic Catholicism," *Hispanic Catholic Culture in the US: Issues and Concerns*, Allan Figueroa Deck, SJ and Jay P. Dolan, eds. (Notre Dame: University of Notre Dame, 1994), 413–25.

32. Jay P. Dolan, "Conclusion," *Hispanic Catholic Culture*, 455.

33. Moises Sandoval, "The Organization of a Hispanic Church," *Hispanic Catholic Culture*, 163.

34. Boerio-Goates, "The Catholic Church," 19.

35. Andres Tapia, "White-Bread Congregation in D.C. Boils Down to an Asian-Creole Mix Stew," *Salt Lake Tribune*, 23 April 1994, E4.

36. Monsivais, "Our Respective Lands of Jershon," 53–54.

37. Ignacio Garcia, Conversation with author, 11 April 1997, transcript in the Charles Redd Center for Western Studies, Brigham Young University.

38. Esmeralda Meraz, Oral History, interviewed by Jessie Embry, 1991, 9–10, LDS Hispanic American.

CHAPTER NINE

SOME PERSONAL THOUGHTS

As I have researched ethnic groups in the United States—and especially language congregations—I have discussed my ideas with friends, colleagues, Church members, and even total strangers. It is a topic of universal appeal involving issues of racial tolerance, religious integration, cultural imperialism, and class. The discussion always includes the question: "What do you think is the best arrangement for ethnic members?" Answering that question is always difficult for me because my study has revealed dimensions of complexity. In fact, those for whom the question is easy to answer usually have little experience with ethnic congregations.

It is a position I recognize easily, because my personal experience with ethnic congregations was initially based on simplistic models and analogues. In 1984 when Alan Cherry suggested that I develop an oral history project on African American Mormons, I had studied only Swiss American Mormons and the German-speaking branch in Logan, Utah. As far as I could tell, the interviewees were fully integrated into the Mormon and American lifestyle. Until the 1950s (except during World War I and World War II), the first generation of immigrants had attended German-speaking meetings but were members of geographical English-speaking wards where they often continued to speak in their native language during monthly "testimony" meetings. The second generation, however, learned English. They did not feel the same sense of community at or need for German-speaking meetings.[1]

My sole other experience with non-geographical wards in the United States came at age twenty-four in attending a ward for single Latter-day Saints in Salt Lake City in the late 1970s. Although most of the members were, like me, young, unmarried, and launching careers, there were already strong friendship groups from which I felt excluded. I enjoyed the companionship of another woman who had moved into the ward at about the same time, but in reality our careers, interests, and goals were very different.

When I moved to Provo in 1979, my only visit to a singles ward made me feel quite out of place. Its members did not seem to have a common bond at all other than singleness. So when the elders' quorum presidency from the geographical ward invited me to attend those meetings, I did. As I met my neighbors, old and young, I decided I liked the "real world" atmosphere. I enjoyed visiting with Irene Carlson, a retired school teacher in her eighties. I liked making cookies with three-year-old Kim and six-year-old Katie Richards. I liked talking about my research with their father, A. LeGrand "Buddy" Richards, a BYU professor, and their mother, Cindy, a former high school sociology teacher. Now I have attended wards with my neighbors for almost twenty years and have many friends with whom I have much in common. This experience reinforced my feeling that the blending of diverse personalities and backgrounds through assignment to geographical wards was the "right" way to organize Mormon groups.

But then in 1985 I had another view of foreign-language speaking congregations. I visited the Richards, then living in Germany, for two weeks. I speak no German. I learned to get around on the bus by watching very closely, I was able to make purchases by pointing, and I practiced saying, "Guten Morgen." Most of the time I was with the Richards, so I did not feel completely isolated. Yet I felt a great sense of belonging when I went to the English-speaking American service ward on Sunday. Its members might not have been my friends in the United States, but I felt an immediate bond with them because we shared the same citizenship, the same language, and the same church in a foreign country where we were the minority. From the background of these personal experiences, then, I began researching ethnic congregations in the United States.

Integrated Wards or Language Branches?

Like Golden Buchanan, I initially supported integrated wards and branches. I felt that to strengthen the Church and to promote better understanding members should worship together. My experience in single wards had convinced me that special-interest segregation was artificial, perhaps even unhealthy. I assumed ethnic branches and wards would have the same problems.

Alan Cherry agreed. He had returned to New York City in the late 1960s after joining the LDS Church in Texas. The New York World's Fair, just concluded, had successfully attracted many Spanish-speaking converts. He was disappointed when they were grouped into the newly created Manhattan Spanish American Branch. They were enthusiastic converts: and when they left, Cherry felt they took part of the ward's life. He had hoped members would learn Spanish and interact with the converts. Cherry also questioned the purpose for continuing Genesis, a group for African Americans, after the priesthood revelation in 1978.[2]

Naturally, the question—separate or integrated—was high on the list of discussion topics when the Redd Center started the LDS Hispanic American Oral History Project. Esmeralda Meraz, a Mexican American interviewer, had attended both English- and Spanish-speaking congregations in Southern California. I quote her views of the strengths and weaknesses of these units frequently. While she clearly felt that the Spanish-speaking branch helped her parents who spoke little or no English, she had mixed feelings for herself. She liked the completeness of the program in the English-speaking wards, yet sometimes felt excluded by some European Americans. She enjoyed the enthusiasm and warm companionship in the Spanish-speaking congregation, but disliked the small branch where there were very few youth.

In 1996 I visited Meraz, then living near Washington, D.C., and working for a U.S. Senate committee. She and her husband, an Anglo American law student who had served a Spanish-speaking mission attended a geographical ward. They felt accepted and comfortable, but Meraz reported that the workers in the Washington, D.C., Temple often encouraged her to go to the Spanish-speaking branch to help "her people." Meraz resented the assumption that she could serve only in a Spanish-speaking setting.

As the oral history project with ethnic members continued, I became less convinced that integrated wards were the best answer—especially for people like Meraz's parents. Integrated wards might be the most comfortable for English-speaking Americans like me. They might be the easiest for Church leaders—local and General Authorities—to administer. But what is best for the individual members?[3]

Oddly enough, when I began asking the question in this way, I realized that the decision-making process itself may work against being able to find the answer because individuals do not make the decision. In the Church, leaders make the decisions—sometimes on the local level, but often on the general or regional level, sometimes with member input and sometimes without it. Frequently after the decision is made, there is no way to appeal it if members feel that it does not fit their circumstances. In Provo I had the option of attending a neighborhood ward or a singles ward. The constant cycle of creating singles wards yet periodically expelling everyone who does not fit within certain age parameters is probably the example with which most LDS members are familiar.

Ideally, ethnic members also have the choice to attend an ethnic or geographical ward or branch. But in some locales, if a program exists or does not exist for a group, members are required to adjust to the situation. For example, a Navajo living in Shiprock, New Mexico, wanted to attend a largely Navajo ward in the neighboring town of Kirtland. But the stake president complained and would not allow her to have church positions in the Kirtland ward.

An additional concern is what programs work best in ethnic congregations? The assumption of leaders is that the standard program of the Church, created and implemented fully, is the best program. The Basic Unit Program showed at least one example where General Authorities agreed that the standard program needed to be adjusted for small groups. But usually all wards and branches in the Church run basically the same. This helps in administration, but does it meet all the needs of the members? Since this is not a unique concern for Mormons, how have others dealt with the same issue?

Sociologists' Views

Throughout history, race, ethnicity, and religion have regularly created barriers among citizens of nations. Especially where physical and cultural differences were noticeable, one group has typically dominated, and the subordinate group has often been segregated, that is, separated physically at home, at work, and at social activities. Attempts to eliminate segregation have taken several routes, including (1) assimilation, "the process by which a subordinate individual or group takes on the characteristics of the dominant group and is eventually accepted as part of the group"; (2) cultural pluralism, "mutual respect between various groups in a society . . . that allow[s] minorities to express their own culture without suffering prejudice or hostility"; and (3) fusion, "a minority and a majority group combining to form a new group." Fusion has taken place on a small scale in some countries, but in the United States, the so-called melting pot, the dominant group has preferred assimilation and at best only tolerated cultural pluralism.[4]

In an ideal world, fusion and not assimilation would be the pattern. I would learn to speak Spanish (and many other languages) and be able to communicate with Latino American Mormons. I would learn something about their culture and accept any differences just as they would accept my world view. But realistically, I acknowledge that I have abandoned my attempts to learn Spanish before I have mastered the language and understanding someone else's world view is harder than I thought.

LDS Views

For these reasons (along with many others), Mormons have also usually supported assimilation. Nineteenth-century Swedish immigrants were told to leave behind their culture and "adopt the manners and customs of the American people, fit themselves to become good and loyal citizens of this country, and by their good works show that they [were] true and faithful Latter-day Saints."[5] Ethnic congregations—whether organized in the nineteenth or twentieth century—were seen as temporary measures until the newcomers could learn English and fit into a geographical ward. To use Latino historian and former Mormon bishop Ignacio Garcia's term, such wards were the "minor leagues."

Spencer W. Kimball as a Case Study

Apostle and later Church President Spencer W. Kimball epitomized the dilemma facing many LDS Church leaders. Unlike some of his co-workers, Kimball strongly supported ethnic congregations. But he also considered them to be temporary homes until the members could fit into the geographical wards. Furthermore, he supported some integration at all times; he asked the members of the Spanish-speaking branches in the West Spanish American Mission to remain in geographical stakes rather than being part of the language mission.

Kimball also was unsure about the importance of ethnic culture to individual identity. In his work with Native Americans, he encouraged ethnic parents to teach their culture and language to their children. He supported cultural activities in the language branches. But, like others of his generation, he often expressed his pleasure at how Native Americans adapted to what he considered accepted behavior. After a 1963 visit to the Southwest Indian Mission, he praised "the progress of the Indians." He recalled, "When I began coming to this area, the Indians were backward and timid and frightened. When we approached them, they stayed off, hid their faces, stood like a post."[6] He recorded after a district conference in Kayenta in 1962, "It was thrilling indeed to see the beginning of what will become standard procedure in the future with Indian leaders in branches and districts, Indians at the piano, at the baton, Indians at the pulpit, Indians making the arrangements, Indians even furnishing the luncheon."[7] Many of these characteristics—taking leadership roles and looking directly at people—went against Navajo beliefs that people should not try to elevate themselves above others and that looking directly into people's eyes is rude.

Yet despite these weaknesses, Kimball was more willing to accept other cultures than many other English-speaking American Mormons. George P. Lee, a Navajo and former LDS General Authority, explained Kimball "assisted many Indians to acquire self-regard in their native culture as well as in the dominant white culture in order to transcend both."[8]

My Experience

After researching LDS African Americans, LDS Native Americans, LDS Hispanic Americans, LDS Asian Americans, and LDS Polynesian Americans, I better understand Kimball's dilemmas. While I see virtue in ethnic and language congregations, I also hope for a day when, as Jerri Hale Harwell, an LDS African American, explained, for everyone to be seen as children of God.[9] While I see cultural differences, my world view is restricted by my European American upbringing. The difference is that I am now aware of the ways in which my own culture limits and restricts me, even as it simultaneously supports and privileges me.

So I find it difficult to answer the question whether language congregations should or should not continue in the United States. I am no longer the integrationist that I was when started out, but I am not convinced that always having separate congregations is the best answer.

Part of the reason for that is that no one answer meets the needs of all ethnic members. A immigrant grandmother may need activities in a ward which are similar to those of her homeland. She may need to associate with women her own age who share her experience. Her children may need direct language tutoring, orientation in community programs, employment guidance and training, and networking skills to function in an English-speaking society. But they may also need a place where they can maintain their native language and culture. Their children often have assimilated into the dominant culture, but they need to be taught respect and appreciation for the family traditions. These generational concerns complicate how the Church deals with ethnic members.

I do agree with Ignacio Garcia that the best decisions are made on the local level. As ward/branch and stake leaders and members work together, they can determine what works best for their congregations. The strengths and weaknesses described in this book will provide a common vocabulary and create a history of shared memory so that the cycles of experimentation, creation, and retrenchment may encourage innovation, waste less time, and better match institutional resources with individual needs. We can also learn from the experience of religious, community, government, and business groups. Flexible solutions, such as the Church's Basic Unit Plan, can help in meeting the needs of individual members while maintaining the organizational structure.

Notes

1. For information on the German-speaking meetings in Logan, see Jessie L. Embry, "Little Berlin: Swiss Saints of the Logan Tenth Ward," *Utah Historical Quarterly* 56 (Summer 1988): 222–235.

2. For more information on Genesis Groups and the experiences of African Americans, see Jessie L. Embry, "Separate but Equal? Black Branches, Genesis Groups, or Integrated Wards," *Dialogue: A Journal of Mormon Thought* 23 (Spring 1990): 11–37.

3. For information which compares the responses of Native Americans and Hispanic members, see Jessie L. Embry, "Ethnic Groups and the LDS Church," *Dialogue: A Journal of Mormon Thought* 25 (Winter 1992): 82–97.

4. Richard T. Schaefer, *Racial and Ethnic Groups* (Glenville, IL: Scott, Foreman, and Co., 1988), 20, 36, 40, 38–39.

5. Quoted in Stephen Cameron McCracken, "German-Speaking Immigrants Living in Cache Valley: An Oral History" (M.A. thesis, Utah State University, 1986), 107.

6. Spencer W. Kimball Journal, 23 April 1963, in private possession. Used by permission of the family.

7. Ibid., June 3, 1962; Golden R. Buchanan, Oral History, interviewed by William G. Hartley, April 1975, 4:131, LDS Church Archives, Historical Department, Church of Jesus Christ of Latter-day Saints, Salt Lake City, Utah.

8. George P. Lee, *Silent Courage: An Indian Story* (Salt Lake City: Deseret Book, 1987), 340.

9. Embry, "Separate but Equal," 34.

APPENDIX ONE

HISPANIC AMERICAN ORAL HISTORIES CODING FORM

Country

Gender

Age

Religious background

Role of religion

Family status

Family activities

Economic background
- Father
- Mother
- Self
- In home country
- In U.S.

Educational level

Conversion
- In native country
- U.S.

First Contact with Mormons
- Missionaries
  - English class
  - Street
  - Door to door
  - World fair
- Friends
- Family
- Members

Age at conversion

Family reaction

Changes in lifestyle after joining LDS Church

Description of LDS Church in native country

Immigration
- Reasons
- First impressions
- Language

Relationships with European Americans
- General
- School
- Work

Key friendships with European Americans

Advantages of living in U.S.

Disadvantages of living in U.S.

Relationships with other ethnic groups

Maintaining culture in the U.S.
- Holidays
- Food
- Others

Relationships with LDS European Americans
- General
- Church
- Out of church

Seen by LDS European Americans as
- Individual
- Member of an ethnic group

Actions of European American Mormons that bother LDS Latino Americans

Ethnic congregation
- Attendance at a Spanish-speaking ward or branch
  - Yes
  - No

Description of Spanish-speaking ward or branch

Feelings about attending a Spanish-speaking ward or branch
- Positive
- Negative
- Mixed

Advantages of Spanish-speaking wards and branches

Disadvantages of Spanish-speaking wards and branches

Ward activities

Views of dating in the United States
- Date LDS
- Date Latinos
- Date LDS and Latinos
- Marriage
- Marital status

Children
- Yes
- No

Values important to teach children
- LDS
- Ethnic

Important LDS programs to share with children

Children acceptance by LDS European Americans
- Accepted church/community
- Accepted church
- Accepted community
- Children are discriminated against
- Sense prejudice

Outlook of missionary work

Cultural differences between American and Latino values

Cultural difference Mormon and Latino values

APPENDIX TWO

CHARLES REDD CENTER FOR WESTERN STUDIES LDS HISPANIC ORAL HISTORY INTERVIEWS

INTERVIEWEE	INTERVIEWER	DATE	LOCATION OF INTERVIEW
Abaroa, Josie	Andrea Van Wagenen	24 Nov. 1991	Provo, UT
Aguila, Maria	Katuska Serrano	29 Aug. 1991	Sepulveda, CA
Aguila, Victor	Katuska Serrano	16 Sept. 1991	Provo, UT
Andrade, Teresa	Katuska Serrano	21 Aug. 1991	Palcolma, CA
Arcia, Joaquin	Katuska Serrano	28 Dec. 1991	Glendale, CA
Arciniega, Rebecca E.	Katuska Serrano	11 Oct. 1991	Provo, UT
Ayerdis, Roberto	Janean Baker	8 Oct., 1992 5 Nov. 1992	Andrews Air Force Base, MD
Barreto, Dalva	Katuska Serrano	26 Aug. 1991	Van Nuys, CA
Black, Lorena	Katuska Serrano	27 Aug. 1991	Panorama City, CA
Cabrera, Angela	Katuska Serrano	25 Dec. 1991	Glendale, CA
Calderwood, Ines	Andrea Van Wagenen	26, 27 Oct. 1991	Provo, UT
Camargo, Elena	Katuska Serrano	12 Sept. 1991	Provo, UT
Cetina, Carlos	Katuska Serrano	30 Dec. 1991	Los Angeles, CA
Cetina, Marse	Katuska Serrano	30 Dec. 1991	Los Angeles, CA
Chong, Johnny	Katuska Serrano	21 Dec. 1991	Glendale, CA
Cifuentes, Nestor	Andrea Van Wagenen	26 Oct. 1991	Provo, UT
Conde, Marisol	Katuska Serrano	28 Dec. 1991	Glendale, CA
Cordon, Max	Katuska Serrano	30 July 1991	Provo, UT
Cortez, Enrique	Katuska Serrano	23 Aug. 1991	San Fernando Valley, CA
D'Ambrosio, Ricardo	Andrea Van Wagenen	28 Jan. 1992	Salt Lake City, UT
De La O, Marta	Katuska Serrano	27 Dec. 1991	La Cresenta, CA
de Luna, Raquel	Katuska Serrano	21 Aug. 1991	Sepulveda, CA
Diaz, Ricardo	Esmeralda Meraz	13 Mar. 1991	Provo, UT
Diaz, Marco	Katuska Serrano	19 July 1991	Provo, UT
Diaz, Ricardo	Esmeralda Meraz	13 Mar. 1991	Provo, UT
Escarzaga, Alva Luz	Katuska Serrano	20 Sept. 1991	Provo, UT

INTERVIEWEE	INTERVIEWER	DATE	LOCATION OF INTERVIEW
Escolar, Gregorio	Katuska Serrano	19 July 1991	Provo, UT
Espinel, Edwin	Esmeralda Meraz	22 Mar. 1991	Provo, UT
Espinoza, Luis	Andrea Van Wagenen	19 Feb. 1992	Provo, UT
Flores, Enoc Q	Esmeralda Meraz	18, 26 Mar. 1991	Provo, UT
Fuentes, Arlene	Andrea Van Wagenen	23 Feb. 1992	Provo, UT
Furrows, Myriam Lopez	Katuska Serrano	3 July 1991	Provo, UT
Garcia, Norman	Katuska Serrano	9 July 1991	Provo, UT
Garcia, Juan Luis	Katuska Serrano	23 July 1991	Provo, UT
Gigena, Marcelo Alfredo	Katuska Serrano	10 Oct. 1991	Provo, UT
Giuria, Gustavo	Katuska Serrano	24 Aug. 1991	Panorama City, CA
Gonzales, Kenneth	Esmeralda Meraz	20 Mar. 1991	Provo, UT
Guajardo, Francisco	Andrea Van Wagenen	17 Nov. 1991	Provo, UT
Herrera, Pilar	Andrea Van Wagenen	23 Nov. 1991	Provo, UT
Hoskisson, Quina	Esmeralda Meraz	5 Apr. 1991 5 Nov 1991	Provo, UT
Jenks, Cristina	Katuska Serrano	27 Dec. 1991	Glendale, CA
Keetch, Yvonne	Katuska Serrano	30 July 1991 6 Aug. 1991	Provo, UT
Landaverde, Maritza	Katuska Serrano	26 Aug. 1991	Sepulveda, CA
Lara, Zenon	Katuska Serrano	21 Dec. 1991	Glendale, CA
Linares, William	Katuska Serrano	28 Dec. 1991	Glendale, CA
Lom, Imelda	Andrea Van Wagenen	5 Feb. 1992	Provo, UT
Lombardo, Noemí	Katuska Serrano	20, 21 Aug. 1991	Van Nuys, CA
Lopez, Adriana A.	Katuska Serrano	29 July 1991	Provo, UT
Mejia, Gaudencio	Andrea Van Wagenen	16 Nov. 1991	Provo, UT
Mena, Delmy	Katuska Serrano	30 Aug. 1991	Van Nuys, CA
Meraz, Rosalinda	Esmeralda Meraz	15 May 1991	El Centro, CA
Meraz, Esmeralda	Jessie L. Embry	7 Mar. 1991	Provo, UT
Morales, Lidi	Andrea Van Wagenen	3 Feb. 1992	Provo, UT
Morales, Dioni	Andrea Van Wagenen	5 Feb. 1992	Provo, UT
Moreno, Gloria	Esmeralda Meraz	27 Apr. 1991	Watsonville, CA
Nelson, Maria Lepe	Katuska Serrano	22 Aug. 1991	Arleta, CA
Ovando, Hector	Katuska Serrano	2 Jan. 1992	Los Angeles, CA
Ovando, Rita Eugenia	Katuska Serrano	26 Dec. 1991	Los Angeles, CA
Ovando, Lidia	Katuska Serrano	29 Aug. 1991	Sepulveda, CA
Piña, Juan	Katuska Serrano	26 Aug. 1991	Van Nuys, CA

INTERVIEWEE	INTERVIEWER	DATE	LOCATION OF INTERVIEW
Quiroz, Lidia	Katuska Serrano	25 Sept. 1991	Provo, UT
Ramirez, Consuelo	Katuska Serrano	28 Aug. 1991	Van Nuys, CA
Ramirez, Francisco	Katuska Serrano	19 Aug. 1991	Van Nuys, CA
Ramos, Pavel	Andrea Van Wagenen	10 Dec. 1991	Provo, UT
Rodriguez, Bricia Z.	Andrea Van Wagenen	4 Oct. 1991	Provo, UT
Rodriguez, Victor	Andrea Van Wagenen	10 Oct. 1991	Provo, UT
Rojas, Burton A.	Esmeralda Meraz	4 Apr. 1991	Provo, UT
Rubio, José	Esmeralda Meraz	16 Apr. 1991	Provo, UT
Ruvalcaba, Dinah	Katuska Serrano	19 Sept. 1991	Provo, UT
Sanchez, Ivan	Katuska Serrano	1 Oct. 1991	Provo, UT
Sarrazin, Alfredo	Katuska Serrano	19 July 1991	Provo, UT
Serrano, Patricia	Katuska Serrano	28 Aug. 1991	Glendale, CA
Serrano, Katuska	Jessie L. Embry	25 June 1991	Provo, UT
Serrano, Tina T.	Katuska Serrano	18 Sept. 1991	Provo, UT
Silvas-Ayerdis, Esperanza	Janean Baker	19 Nov. 1992	Andrews Air Force Base, MD
Sosa, Sergio Fernando	Katuska Serrano	2 Aug. 1991	Orem, UT
Spannaus, Alin	Katuska Serrano	28 Oct. 1991	Provo, UT
Tirado, Carlos	Katuska Serrano	13 Sept. 1991	Provo, UT
Ulloa, Sara	Katuska Serrano	2 Aug. 2, 1991	Provo, UT
Valdivieso, Elizabeth	Katuska Serrano	21 Aug. 21, 1991	Van Nuys, Ca
Valdivieso, Marco	Katuska Serrano	23 Aug. 23, 1991	Van Nuys, CA
Valencia, Mario	Esmeralda Meraz	17 Apr. 1991	Provo, UT
Vallota, Enrique Hugo	Andrea Van Wagenen	20 Oct. 1991	Los Angeles, CA
Vallota, Stella Maris	Andrea Van Wagenen	22 Sept. 1991	Los Angeles, CA
Van Wagenen, Andrea	Jessie L. Embry	16 Sept. 1991	Provo, UT
Vargas, Miguel	Katuska Serrano	29 Aug. 1991	Van Nuys, CA
Vargas, Rina	Katuska Serrano	27 Aug. 1991	Van Nuys, CA
Vernardi, Agripina	Esmeralda Meraz	4 May 1991	El Centro, CA
Vigil, Steven Chris	Katuska Serrano	19 July 1991	Provo, UT
Yapias, Adolfo Tony	Katuska Serrano	11 July 1991	Provo, UT
Zaldaña, María	Katuska Serrano	27 Aug. 1991	Van Nuys, CA
Zamarron, Lorenza	Katuska Serrano	30 July 1991 9 Sept. 1991	Provo, UT
Zambrano, Adenaver	Katuska Serrano	10 Sept. 1991	Provo, UT
Zavala, Martha	Katuska Serrano	16 July 1991	Provo, UT

INDEX